Although the Imperial Russian Army experimented with an unsuccessful tank design known as the Tsar Tank in 1916, operational tanks did not make their appearance in Russia until 1919, when the British and French supplied small numbers of Mk V and Renault FT tanks to the Loyalist forces during the Russian Civil War. Both types saw limited action in the north and south, the two main fronts where Allied intervention forces were in action on the Loyalist side against the Bolsheviks. One of the most dramatic actions occurred on 30 June 1919, when a single Mk V commanded by a British officer, Major Ewen Cameron Bruce, drove into the city of Tsaritsyn, causing panic among the defending Bolsheviks and bringing about their surrender.

The effectiveness of the tank demonstrated in this action and others on the Petrograd Front, was not lost on the Bolsheviks who, ultimately victorious in the Civil War, lost no time in creating an armoured force. Such a force had in fact existed on paper since January 1918 as a department of the embryo Red Army, and as the Civil War drew to a close it made use of a number of captured Vickers and FT tanks, together with some Austin armoured cars, abandoned by the Allied Intervention Forces. Numbers of Renault FT tanks were used in the Russo-Polish war of 1919–21, a conflict that underlined the need for a strong armoured force capable of penetrating enemy defensive lines.

After relying on foreign tank imports (mainly French FT-17s) for some time, the new Soviet government, established in 1922, gave high priority to the creation of tank design and production facilities, and to this end a Tank Bureau was formed in May 1924 to oversee the development of indigenous Soviet tanks. In the same year the Bureau issued a specification for a light infantry support vehicle, a three-ton two-man tank with 16mm of armoured protection and fitted with a 37mm main gun. An unusual feature was the turret armament arrangement, in which the 37mm main armament and the machine gun were offset at 45° to one another.

Based on the Renault FT and powered by a 35hp engine of Fiat design, the first prototype was designated T-16, which emerged as the T-18 after some improvements to the engine and hull design had been incorporated. The first prototype bore the manufacturer's designation MS-1 which stood for *Maliy Soprovozdiniya* (Small Support Vehicle) Type 1.

The T-18 was the first operational armoured fighting vehicle of Soviet design, and although it suffered from many inadequacies, including being underpowered and under-gunned, it nevertheless gave the Russians experience in tank design and construction which they had previously lacked. The prototype was built in 1928 and entered service in the following year. Production, which was undertaken by the Leningrad Bolshevik Plant (Factory 232,

formerly the Obukhov State Plant) e 1931. After its withdrawal from fr service in 1932, the T-18 was alloc military training units.

Although incorporating feature were not present in the FT-17, the T-18 was still essentially a copy of the French tank, while the T-26, produced in large numbers in the Soviet Union from 1930, was a faithful copy of the British Vickers 6-ton light tank. Not only did it provide a substantial nucleus of Russian tank men with practical experience of operating what was then a modern armoured fighting vehicle, it also led directly to many improvements that would be incorporated in later generations of Soviet AFVs. But the T-26 was still a foreign design, and it was not until the appearance of the 29-ton T-28 in 1931 that the Red Army could claim to field a tank that was truly Russian in concept.

The prototype was armed with a 45mm gun, which was replaced by a 76mm weapon in the first production model, the T-28A, which was issued to Soviet armoured units from 1933. The next production variant, the T-28B, which made its appearance in 1938, featured a new long-barrelled 76mm weapon with a better performance. The main armament was housed in one large turret that was flanked by two smaller ones housing machine guns, an arrangement that was fashionable in the early 1930s. All T-28s were equipped with radio, which was mostly lacking in the tanks of other nations at that time, and had mounts for anti-aircraft machine guns. The T-28's participation in the Winter War of 1939–40, when it suffered grievous losses to Finnish anti-tank weaponry, revealed the inadequacy of its armour, which was upgraded in a series of hastily implemented programmes.

Despite its deficiencies, the T-28 was the world's first mass-produced medium tank, and the vehicle that set Russian tank designers on the road that would lead to the T-34.

The large, unwieldy Tsar Tank, developed from 1914, used a tricycle design featuring two massive front wheels and a smaller rear wheel instead of tracks. Trials showed it to be underpowered and vulnerable, and it was abandoned.

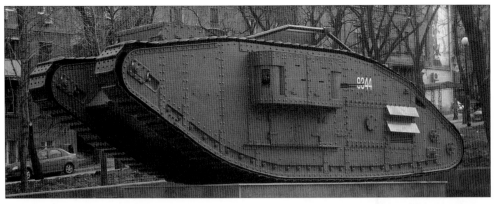

Numbers of British and French tanks were used by both sides in the Russian Civil War. This British Vickers Mk V is preserved at Kharkov in the Ukraine.

The T-28 multi-turreted tank was one of the world's first medium tanks, and was an infantry support vehicle designed to break through fortified defences. This T-28E is pictured at the Parola Tank Museum, Finland. (Balcer, public domain)

The Vickers A1E1 was produced only as a prototype, but its multi-turreted configuration influenced other designs such as the Soviet T-35 heavy tank, which was built in limited numbers. (Bovington Tank Museum)

A T-26 Model 1933 at the museum 'Breaching of the Leningrad Blockade' near Kirovsk, Leningrad Oblast. This tank was raised from a river bottom at Nevsky Pyatachok in May 2003.

The MS-1, seen here at the Moscow Museum of Armed Forces, was the prototype of the T-18 and was the first Soviet-designed tank, although it was based on the Renault FT17. It was in production from 1928 to 1931.

The Vickers E tank, also known as the Vickers 6-tonner, was the vehicle on which the Soviet T-26 was based.

The Renault FT17 was probably the best light tank of its day, and was widely used by a number of countries, including the USSR.

Development and Design

The inauguration of the first Soviet Five Year Plan in 1928 brought with it clearer definitions and more precise aims in matters of economy, industry and defence, the principal requirement being to achieve more Soviet self-sufficiency and independence from foreign imports. Nevertheless, reliance on foreign aid and ideas remained an important factor for some years to come, and in this respect a leading role was played by Amtorg, a Soviet trade organization that had been set up in New York in 1924. Amtorg's function was to secure imports of all kinds on behalf of the new communist regime, and in 1930 its agents began to show considerable interest in a tank developed by an American automotive engineer, J. Walter Christie.

Christie's tank design, the three-man T3 (M1931), was significant because of its suspension, an ingenious arrangement of springs and large road wheels that permitted a considerable vertical wheel displacement when moving at speed over rough ground. There was a penalty in that the undulating movement of the tank at speed made accurate firing on the

move impossible, but the concept of the fast tank was attractive, and the Amtorg agents used their political contacts in New York to persuade US military and civilian officials to provide plans and specifications of the Christie tank to the Soviet Union. At least two of Christie's tanks, minus turrets, were later purchased in the United States and sent to the Soviet Union under false documentation, in which they were described as agricultural tractors. The vehicles were extensively tested at the Voronezh tank training area in 1931, after which they were delivered to the Kharkov Komintern Locomotive Plant (KhPZ, renamed Factory No. 183 in 1936) and arrangements made to produce a Russian copy.

The original Christie tanks were given the designation BT-1 (Bystrokhodny Tank, or High Speed Tank) and formed the basis for three unarmed prototypes of a production version, the BT-2, which was the first of the BT series of so-called cavalry tanks produced in large numbers between 1932 and 1941. The original production BT-2 was armed with a 37mm Model 1930 main gun

The Christie T3 tank and its crew. The purchase of the blueprints by Soviet agents was inspired. (Harris & Ewing Collection, Library of Congress)

The Christie tank's novel suspension enabled the vehicle to perform manoeuvres that were beyond the capability of other armoured vehicles. Here, a Christie T3E2 is being put through its paces. (Harris & Ewing Collection, Library of Congress)

and a 7.62mm DT machine gun, although in later models the main armament was upgraded to a 45mm 1932 gun.

The BT tanks were known as convertible tanks, the Christie design incorporating a feature intended to reduce wear of the unreliable tank tracks of the 1930s. In about thirty minutes, the crew could remove the tracks and engage a chain drive to the rearmost road wheel on each side, allowing the tank to travel at very high speeds on roads. In wheeled mode, the tank was steered by pivoting the front road wheels. Soviet tank forces soon found the convertible option of little practical use; in a country with few paved roads, it consumed space and added needless complexity and weight. The feature was dropped from later Soviet designs. Another feature, adopted by Christie and retained in the Soviet derivatives, was sloping front hull armour, or glacis plate, which minimized the effect of anti-tank projectiles. Sloping side armour was also later to become a standard fitting in Soviet tank turret designs.

The ultimate Soviet derivation of Christie's design was the BT-7, which incorporated numerous improvements and entered service with the Red Army in 1935. The BT tanks were fast and manoeuvrable, although these attributes were only achieved at the expense of armour, the lack of which made the tanks vulnerable. Some BT tanks

The Christie design was developed into the BT series of tanks by Soviet engineers. Known as cavalry tanks, they were produced in large numbers.

Right: The BT-5 was a much improved version of the BT tank series, but still lacked adequate armour and firepower. This example, preserved as a museum piece, is bedecked with flowers in memory of Soviet tank men who lost their lives.

Below: Soviet BT tanks preparing for action at Khalkhin Gol, on the Soviet–Manchurian frontier, in 1939. (Source unknown, via J.R. Cavanagh)

Soviet troops advancing at Khalkhin Gol, supported by a BT-7 tank. (Courtesy of Anthony Tucker-Jones)

were tested under operational conditions in the Spanish Civil War and were used during the Russo-Finnish war in 1939–40, where they suffered heavy losses to Finnish anti-tank weapons. The earlier BT tanks also saw service in the Far East, where the Soviet Union became embroiled in border incidents with Japanese forces occupying Manchuria in the late 1930s. These conflicts underlined the vulnerability of the BT series, with their inadequate armour protection and petrol-driven M-5 engines, which were prone to catching fire. An engine fire would

quickly spread to the main body of the tank via gaps in the armour plating. The rivets that held the vehicle together also presented a problem in that a projectile strike would cause them to spring, turning them into lethal wasps that tore round the interior of the crew compartment.

The last version of the BT-7 was the BT-7M, also known as the BT-8, which was fitted with a new V-2 diesel engine. In all, the Kharkov Locomotive Factory produced some 8,000 BT tanks of all variants in the decade from 1928 to 1938, when a department was formed to design a new medium tank that incorporated all the operational lessons of the Soviet fighting vehicles that had gone before. Design leadership of the department was assigned to a talented 40-year-old engineer called Mikhail Ilyich Koshkin, a graduate of the Leningrad Polytechnic Institute, where he specialized in tank design. On graduation he joined the S.M. Kirov Factory 185 in Leningrad, where he became involved in a number of tank design projects. These included the T-29 battle tank project, work on which was halted when Koshkin was called to Kiev in November 1937, and the T-111 medium tank. Koshkin lost no time in recruiting the most talented of his colleagues, including Alexander Morozov, his principal assistant, and Nikolai Kucherenko, who became production manager.

Pooling all the experience of earlier designs, Koshkin and his team set about designing a completely new medium tank, designated A-20. The design specification called for a vehicle fitted with the Christie-type wheel-and-track propulsion system, 20mm of armour protection, and a 45mm main gun. Koshkin and his colleagues were dubious about the value of the wheel-and-track system; the concept of a tank that could run on wheels alone had worked reasonably well in the earlier 1930s, when track failure was a frequent occurrence, but since then there had been much progress in track design, and the effectiveness of – or need for – a dual system was questionable.

Left: The crew of a Soviet BT tank surrendering to a Japanese officer at Khalkhin Gol. (Source unknown, via J.R. Cavanagh)

Below: The A-20 medium tank was developed by pooling all the design expertise gained with the BT series and other tank projects that never came to fruition. Improving the design of the tank tracks was a major concern. (Kharkov Machine Building Design Bureau, public domain)

Early in 1938, the design team from the Kharkov Factory No. 183 attended a meeting of the Military Council in Moscow in which the assistant commander for technical affairs of the International Tank Regiment, Aleksandr Vetrov, was questioned about his experiences in Spain. The design team came away from the meeting further reinforced in their view that the specification for the design of the new fast tank was ill-conceived. The team's conviction was that the new fast tank should have thicker armour to protect it against a new generation of anti-tank weapons that would be even more effective than the German 37mm gun encountered in Spain, and should have a heavier main gun than the 45mm armament of the T-26 and BT.

Despite all the evidence presented by the experts, General Dmitry Pavlov, at that time head of the Directorate of Tank and Armoured Car Troops of the Red Army, decreed that the existing specification should stand. A wooden mock-up of the A-20 was therefore built according to the specification and examined by the Defence Committee of the Council of People's Commissars (SNK). It was at this point that Soviet leader Josef Stalin stepped in and made a vital decision. Having assessed the evidence in support of a much-upgraded design, he overruled the Armoured Forces Directorate and decreed that the new tank should use only tracked propulsion, have 30mm of protection and be fitted with a 76mm main gun.

Right: The two
dictators, Stalin and
Hitler. Both interfered
with the production
of armaments for
their respective
armed forces.
(Source unknown, via
J.R. Cavanagh)

Left: Voroshilov was
replaced as People's
Commissar for Defence
by Marshal Semyon
Timoshenko, who
quickly set about re-
forming the mechanized
corps and establishing
new ones. (Novosti)

Two prototypes of the new tank were authorized, the first of these – the A-20 according to the specification – and the second, originally designated A-30 but soon redesignated A-32, with the upgraded features. The A-20 prototype used existing parts of the BT-7 and BT-7M and was fitted with three pairs of driving wheels, of which only the first pair was steerable. The turret, using parts taken from the BT-7 and BT-SV, mounted a 45mm 20K gun. The armour protection was sloped at angles varying between 20mm and 25mm and the tracks were 400mm wide, much wider than the 263mm of the BT-7 series, which greatly improved both mobility and stability. It weighed 18 tons.

The A-20 was completed in May 1939 and the other prototype, the A-32, in July. A ton heavier than the A-20, the A-32 had the same 500hp V-2 diesel engine but was fitted with an extra pair of driving wheels, which made for better weight distribution. Main armament was the 76mm L-10 gun. Like the A-20, the A-32 had a four-man crew.

In August 1939 both prototypes were sent to the Research Institute and Proving Grounds of the Armoured Force at Kubinka, near Moscow for comparative trials. These revealed that the maximum speed of both vehicles on tracks was similar – around 40mph – but that in wheeled mode the A-20's cross-country performance was inferior to that of the A-32. The V-2 diesel engine installed in both vehicles performed well. Various recommendations were made, including the possibility of upgrading the A-32's armour. At the conclusion of the trials the tanks were put on display for the benefit of the Main Military Council and senior Red Army officers, but when

they returned to Kharkov on 1 September there was still no decision on which vehicle would be ordered into production.

Back at Kharkov, Koshkin and his team decided to concentrate on refining the A-32. Upgrading the armour protection to between 40mm and 45mm would mean a weight increase of seven tons, which in turn would require wider tracks, but the weight penalty and matters associated with it were considered acceptable. Finally, on 19 December 1939, the Defence Committee of the Council of People's Commissars met to make the final decisions on which tanks were to form the core of the future Soviet armoured force. By this time, the Soviet Union was locked in a bitter war with Finland, and the Defence Committee's decision was greatly influenced by the ease with which Soviet T-26 and BT tanks were being destroyed by the new anti-tank weapons in use by the Finnish Army.

The Defence Committee selected three new tanks for production. The first was the 42-ton Klim-Voroshilov KV-1 heavy tank, developed in 1938 as a successor to the T-35 and taking its name from Klimenti Voroshilov, then the Commissar for Defence. The tank was evaluated under operational conditions in the war with Finland, and ordered into production as the KV-1A, with a long-barrel 76.2mm gun. The KV-1's biggest drawback was that it suffered from a lack of mobility, which caused problems on the vast open spaces of the Russian plain. It was at its most useful in forming the spearhead of an armoured attack, when it was used in the nature of a battering ram to break through enemy defences, creating a gap that could then be exploited by fast cruiser tanks.

On the personal orders of Josef Stalin, General Pavlov was overruled and the second prototype of the new medium tank, the A-32, emerged as a much more viable product. It was armed with the L-10 gun developed for the T-28. (Source unknown, via J.R. Cavanagh)

Far left: The vulnerability of the BT tanks is well illustrated by this image of a BT-5, wrecked by an anti-tank shell during the later fighting in Russia. (Bundesarchiv)

Left: Marshal Kliment Voroshilov's decision to disband the Soviet Army's mechanized divisions was seen to be wrong in the wake of Germany's blitzkrieg in Western Europe, and it was soon reversed. (Vintage Image Photos)

The second was the T-40 amphibious light tank, designed for the reconnaissance role and weighing only six tons.

Then there was the A-32 medium tank, the ideal vehicle for exploiting the gaps punched through enemy defences by the KV-1. Two prototypes were ordered by the Defence Committee under the designation T-34, to be followed by an initial production series of 220 vehicles in 1940, with mass production scheduled to begin in 1941. The prototypes were completed in February 1940, and on 5 March Koshkin himself led both vehicles, accompanied by some Voroshilovietz tracked artillery tractors, from Kharkov to Moscow through a heavy snowstorm. On 18 March both T-34s were demonstrated to Stalin, after which one went to the Kubinka Proving Ground and the other was sent to the Soviet-Finnish front for operational trials, although it arrived too late to see any action.

In April and May, both prototypes undertook an arduous 1,250-mile trek from Kharkov to Moscow and back again via Smolensk and Kiev. Koshkin, 'hands on' as always, took part in this himself. During these trials he caught a severe cold, but

elected to forgo medical treatment so that he could carry on with his work. His health deteriorated rapidly, and in June 1940 he was diagnosed with pneumonia. He died on 26 September 1940. In 1942 Koshkin was posthumously awarded with the State Stalin Prize and the Order of the Red Star. Today, a monument to Koshkin and his war-winning T-34 stands in Kharkov.

Koshkin, whose place as leader of the T-34 design team was taken by Alexander Korozov, was too ill to see the rollout of the first production T-34, which also took place in September 1940, shortly before his death. Meanwhile, the Soviet high command had been busily analyzing the events of May and June 1940, when the deadly combination of German armour and air power had brought about the rapid collapse of the Allied armies in France and the Low Countries. As a result of this analysis, the planned T-34 production level was raised from 220 to 600, with 500 units to be built in Kharkov and the rest in Leningrad.

The early production process inevitably revealed some snags which had to be addressed before mass production could really get under way. One of the most

Top right: The KV-1 heavy tank, pictured here in Kirovsk, was ordered into production alongside the lighter and far more manoeuvrable T-34. (WolfDW, public domain)

An analysis of the rapid collapse of the Allied armies in France caused the Soviet high command to increase tank production. France's best tank was the S34 Somua, seen here at the United States Army Ordnance Museum. Many captured examples were used by the Wehrmacht (Mark Pellegrini, public domain)

serious involved the armour plating, which was of poor quality and had to be replaced. The L-11 gun selected as the T-34's main armament also failed to live up to expectations and a much better weapon, the F-34, designed by a team in Gorki, was proposed, but no one was prepared to authorize a change and the first series-produced T-34s were fitted with the L-11.

By the end of 1940 115 T-34s had been produced, and these were issued to various armoured formations. Just a few months earlier there had been no dedicated armoured formations at all in the Red Army. Such formations had existed in the early 1930s, being armed with heavy, medium and light tanks, and by the beginning of 1936 the Red Army had four mechanized corps, six separate mechanized brigades, six separate tank regiments, fifteen mechanized regiments embedded within cavalry divisions, and considerable numbers of tank battalions and companies.

However, an appraisal of Soviet tank operations in the Far East, against Japan, in the Spanish Civil War and in the Winter War with Finland, convinced Marshal Voroshilov, the People's Commissar for Defence, that the existing mechanized formations were too cumbersome, so in December 1939 the decision was taken to disband them and distribute their assets piecemeal among the infantry divisions. This decision was reversed in May 1940, when the German blitzkrieg in Western Europe showed what could be achieved by armour used en masse. Voroshilov was replaced by Marshal Semyon Timoshenko, who in July 1940 set about forming nine new mechanized corps, with an additional twenty to be established from February and March 1941.

The tribulations of the Soviet mechanized units was due in no small measure to the Stalin purges of the late 1930s, which robbed the Red Army of its most able

Left: T-34 armed with the effective F-34 main gun.

Below: A line-up of T-34 prototypes. The example second from the right is armed with the short L-11 gun, soon replaced by the more effective F-34. (Courtesy of Anthony Tucker-Jones)

commanders. Those who replaced them, with few exceptions, possessed little tactical knowledge and had no clear idea of how to handle often unpredictable battlefield situations. The establishment of new armoured formations and equipping them with the latest tanks was one thing; developing the tactics necessary to make them successful was quite another. It was a deficiency that would not be made good for a long time, and it was to cost the Red Army dearly in the early months of the war in the east following the German invasion of June 1941.

General Friedrich von Mellenthin, chief of staff of the Fifth Panzer Army at the end of the war in Europe, writing of the Soviet armour's performance in the early stages of the fighting on the Eastern Front, stated that the 'Russian tank tactics were clumsy and the armour was dissipated over wide fronts ... in particular the lower and middle commands showed little or no understanding or aptitude for armoured warfare. They lacked the daring, the tactical insight, and the ability to make

quick decisions. The initial operations of the tank armies were a complete failure. In tight masses they groped around in the main German battle zone, they moved hesitantly and without any plan. They got in each other's way, they blundered against our anti-tank guns, or after penetrating our front they did nothing to exploit their advantage ...'

However, Mellenthin conceded that if the Soviet tank tactics were at fault, the tank itself was not. In 1941 'The tank arm ... began the war with the great advantage of possessing in the T-34, a model far superior to any tank on the German side ... The Russian tank designers understand their job thoroughly; they cut out refinements and concentrate on essentials – gun power, armour and cross-country performance. During the war their system of suspension was well in advance of Germany and the West.'

Mellinthin's assessment, however, ignored the technical problems that had plagued the T-34 in the early period of its operational deployment.

The T-34 in Detail

The early production T-34, fully equipped, weighed in at 29.2 short tons. Measured from the front of the main armament to the rear of the hull, it was 21.9 feet in length. Width was 9.8 feet and height eight feet. Track width was eighteen inches and ground clearance sixteen inches. It had an operational range of 250 miles and a top speed of 33mph.

The T-34 had the benefit of excellent **armour protection**, its survivability enhanced by the sloped armour design. In the early T-34 models, the main problem was one of quality, especially of the plate joins and welds. There were many chinks and cracks which proved troublesome in heavy rain, allowing water to enter the tank and short out electrical equipment. Another fault was that the cast turret armour of the 1940 and 1941 T-34 models, which replaced the earlier welded armour, was softer than that used in other parts of

Newly completed T-34s, with their crews, loaded on flat cars for transportation to front-line units. (Courtesy of Anthony Tucker-Jones)

T-34s daubed with winter camouflage en route for delivery to front-line units. (Source unknown, via J.R. Cavanagh)

the tank, offering less protection against anti-tank projectiles. The hull armour, on the other hand, was heat-treated to make it very hard. This had the advantage of offering good protection against anti-tank missiles of a calibre equal to or lower than the armour's thickness, but it could produce a spalling effect, whereby metal inside the vehicle might break into chips and fragments following the impact of a projectile and endanger the crew, even if the projectile failed to penetrate. Another factor affecting the T-34's vulnerability was the presence of built-in fuel cells in the sides of the fighting compartment, which if penetrated could lead to an immediate fire and the destruction of the tank.

The early versions of the T-34 mounted the L-11 76.2 **dual-purpose gun**, which could fire high-explosive or armour-piercing rounds. It had a barrel length of 30.5 calibres (meaning that the length was 30.5 multiples of the gun bore), but this was soon replaced by the longer F-34 of 41.2 calibres. Using the standard Soviet anti-tank shell, the guns had respective muzzle velocities of 612 and 655 metres per second. In common with most other armoured forces, the Russians used the Armour-Piercing Ballistic Cap (APBC) shell, the armour-piercing component consisting of a steel shot fitted with a hollow metal cap to improve its aerodynamics. The cap crumpled on striking the target, allowing the steel shot to impact normally.

Soviet tank crews making their first acquaintance with the T-34 soon discovered one drawback: the new tank was not built for comfort. The biggest problem was lack of internal space, a consequence of the vehicle's sloping armour. The hull was divided into four compartments: Driving, Fighting, Engine and Transmission.

The **driving compartment**, situated in the front of the tank, contained side-by-side seats for the driver-mechanic and the machine gunner-wireless operator. Equipment comprised the driving controls, instruments, engine controls and electrical fittings, the machine gun, some of the fighting equipment, a radio set (not fitted in all tanks), three periscopes, control for the rear louvres, two compressed air bottles, spare parts and tools.

The driver-mechanic, seated in the front left of the hull in a cushioned, non-adjustable armchair-type seat also suffered from a lack of adequate vision. Although he had at his fingertips an excellent fighting machine with superb cross-country performance, thanks to its wide track, excellent suspension and large engine,

Factory-fresh T-34 Model 1940 tanks during trials at Kubinka, ready for delivery to their units. (Source unknown, via J.R. Cavanagh)

The T-34's sloping armour gave excellent protection against most anti-tank projectiles. (Source unknown)

he could not use these attributes to best advantage simply because he could not see features ahead such as folds in the ground and other obstacles. The driver also had a periscope, but it proved to be of little use.

Whereas the A-20 prototype – and the earlier BT series tanks – had been fitted with a steering wheel, the T-34 was steered by two levers, controlling the track speeds. Clutch, footbrake and accelerator were mounted from left to right, as in a conventional motor vehicle. Instrumentation was very basic. A panel directly in front of the driver mounted water temperature and oil temperature gauges, both calibrated from 0–125°C, and an oil pressure gauge from 0–15 kilograms per square centimetre. On another panel to the left were a rev counter, showing between 400 and 3,000rpm, a speedometer, an ammeter from 0–50 amps, a voltmeter 0–50 volts, and the starter switch. Starting was electrical, but there was also a compressed air system for use in an emergency. The gearbox had three forward gears and one reverse. The gearbox was unwieldy and changing gear required considerable force, a fact that contributed to driver fatigue. Driver and gunner gained access to their compartment via the hatch in the glacis at the front of the tank. There was also an armoured auxiliary escape hatch let into the vehicle floor at the feet of the gunner. The hull gunner was seated on the driver's

right in a similar armchair. He was in charge of a 7.62mm Degtyarev gas-operated machine gun, originally an infantry weapon developed for tank use some years earlier. It was fed from a 60-round drum-type magazine and was capable of a rate of fire of up to 600 rounds per minute, although 100 rounds per minute was a more realistic figure under operational conditions.

The cramped conditions inside the T-34 seriously restricted movement in the two-man turret, the **fighting compartment**, which housed the tank commander and the loader. The commander in particular had a difficult task, as he was also required to serve as the gunner, having control of the 76.2mm main gun and the co-axial 7.62mm machine gun. The lack of a turret basket that rotated with the turret, meant that the turret crew – whose seats were attached to the turret ring – could only follow the traverse of the gun by squirming in their seats as the gun swung round. The commander therefore had to lay and fire the gun while at the same time trying to keep an overall view of the tactical situation around him, which was virtually impossible. Nine rounds of ammunition were stored in ready-use racks on the sides of the fighting compartment; once these had been expended the loader had to rip up rubber matting from the floor to gain access to boxes containing more rounds, of which the tank carried seventy-six in total.

This photograph of a T-34/76 Model 1943 gives an excellent view of the F-34 gun and its mantle. (Poznan Military Museum, public domain)

This image of an abandoned T-34 gives a good idea of the thick and heavy crew hatches. (Courtesy of Anthony Tucker-Jones)

The tank commander's field of view was also strictly limited because of the design of the access hatch, which opened forwards and had only a small slit through which the commander could view the battlefield. He had a traversable periscope, but this was practically useless, having a field of view of only 25°. Soviet tank commanders condemned the turret hatches of early models as heavy and hard to open, but it was not until August 1942 that the designers added a second turret hatch.

For laying the gun the T-34 commander had two sighting systems at his disposal, of which one was a periscope dial sight. This had illuminated graticules, which the gunner centred on the target by means of a knob attached to the eyepiece, the range being set by a second knob below. The co-axial machine gun was controlled similarly. Three ranges were provided: up to 1,000m for the machine gun, 3,600m for armour-piercing shot, and 2,100m for high-explosive rounds. The other system, and the more accurate of the two, was a telescopic sight giving a magnification of x 2.5 and a field of view of about 14°. It also had an illuminated graticule with a knob controlling range scales, one graduated up to 5,000m for the main gun and the other 1,400m for the machine gun. A rubber eye guard and brow guard were provided to give the gunner some protection from the often-violent movement of the tank. The optical systems available to the commander were generally regarded as being excellent.

As well as a hand trigger, the main gun and co-axial MG could be fired by a foot pedal, a spring-loaded device fitted on either side of the gun mounting, the main gun firing pedal on the left and the MG pedal on the right.

Behind the fighting compartment, and separated from it by a bulkhead, was the **engine compartment**, containing the engine, four fuel tanks, radiators, two oil tanks and four accumulators. The underside of the engine compartment was fitted with an access door for the water pump and oil pump, the door being protected by an armoured cover on the outside of the vehicle. There was also an aperture for draining water and three slits for inspecting the suspension. The roof of the engine compartment had a large hatch giving access to the engine.

In the early 1930s the Soviet government had initiated the development of diesel engines for use in both aircraft and military vehicles. The first to appear, in 1931, was the AD-1 (Aviadiesel 1), which as its name implied was an aero-engine. It was a twelve-cylinder four-stroke V-type motor, developing 500hp at 1,600rpm. Development of a version for use in tanks proceeded in parallel. Like the AD-1 it was liquid cooled. Its output was 500hp at 1,800rpm and it was basically similar to the aero-engine, with modifications for hull mounting, fuel and a clutch. The engine emerged as the V-2-34, featuring an aluminium alloy body.

The modified engine, the work of a design team led by Konstantin Chelpan and produced at the Kharkov Locomotive Factory, was first installed in the BT-7M (BT-8) series in 1937, and in the T-34 prototypes two years later. Its introduction was far from trouble-free; for one thing, because of the high viscosity of the fuel at low temperatures, the oil had to be heated to a certain level, which meant placing a small stove under the engine compartment to heat the engine before start-up. Problems created by poor quality in the manufacturing process also led to many breakdowns.

Many of the latter originated in the **transmission compartment**, situated in the rear of the tank. It contained the engine clutch, centrifugal fan, gearbox, steering clutches with brakes, electric starter and two fuel tanks. There were two apertures at the sides of the floor for draining fuel, and an opening under the gearbox for draining oil, this being protected by an external armoured hatch. Air inlet louvres were fitted in the roof of the compartment, above the fan, these being covered by metal netting to keep out foreign bodies. Two plates in the roof gave access to the fuel tanks and filler caps.

The transmission problems in the early-model T-34 were so critical that breakdowns often occurred after the tank had travelled only 120 miles or so. The main source of the trouble was inadequate heat treatment of the cogwheels, which were prone to disintegrate. The problem persisted for at least the first two years of the war on the Eastern Front, prompting the High Command to issue the following 'Stalin Order':

Our armoured forces and their units frequently suffer greater losses through mechanical breakdowns than they do in battle. For example, at Stalingrad Front in six days twelve of our tank brigades lost 326 out of their 400 tanks. Of those about 260 were due to mechanical problems. Many of the tanks were abandoned on the battlefield. Similar instances can be observed on other fronts. Since such a high incidence of mechanical defects is implausible, the Supreme Headquarters sees in it covert sabotage and wrecking by certain elements in the tank crews who try to exploit small mechanical troubles to avoid battle.

Henceforth, every tank leaving the battlefield for alleged mechanical reasons is to be gone over by technicians, and if sabotage is suspected, the crews are to be put into tank penal companies or downgraded to the infantry and put into infantry penal companies.

Turret design: the T-34 Models 1940–1943

The first production model of the T-34, the Model 1940, was fitted with either a cast or welded turret. In 1941, Nitsenko and Buslov developed a new cast turret for the T-34 model 1941 which had thicker 52mm armour, although some T-34s continued to feature a welded turret. The latter's weakest point was the lower chin of the turret front, so this was deleted and a single flat plate of thicker armour welded in its place. The earlier blunt-nosed gun mantlet was also replaced by one that came to a sharp point. The T-34 Main Design Bureau at Nizhni Tagil, headed by Morozov, was now attempting to simplify the tank as much as possible in order to speed up production without impairing its performance, so the T-34 Model 1942 emerged with a much rougher finish. It featured both cast and welded turrets, although the cast turret, with its 60mm armour, predominated. A commander's cupola was added during the Model 1942 production run. The biggest turret design change came with the T-34 Model 1943, which was fitted with a new

The T-34 had an excellent ability to surmount obstacles, but this one clearly presented a problem. (Courtesy of Anthony Tucker-Jones)

hexagonal turret to increase internal space and provide greater crew comfort. It entered production in the closing weeks of 1942 and became the most numerous of the 76mm-armed T-34 models. The turret featured twin roof hatches, making entry and exit much simpler for the commander/gunner and machine gunner. The Germans nicknamed it 'Mickey Mouse' because the twin hatches resembled the cartoon character's ears when in the open position.

The T-34's V-2 engine was developed from an aero-engine and featured an aluminium body in its finalized form. This cutaway engine is on display in the Finnish Tank Museum, Parola.

The Su-85 was a dedicated tank destroyer. This example is seen at the Museum of Polish War Technology, Warsaw. (Supertank 17, public domain)

Statistics:	The T-34/76 Model 1941
Armament:	76.2mm (3in) L/41.2 F-34 rifled gun, two 7.62mm (0.3in) Degtaryev DT MGs (one co-axial, one hull-mounted)
Armour:	47mm (1.89in) (hull front), 65mm (2.56in) (turret front)
Crew:	4
Dimensions:	Length 6.09m (20ft), gun trained forward 6.58m (21ft 7in); Width 2.98m (9ft 9in), Height 2.57m (8ft 5in)
Weight:	31,390kg (30.9 tons)
Powerplant:	V-2-34 4-stroke V-12 diesel, 373kW (500bhp) at 1,800rpm
Speed:	40kph (25mph)
Range:	432km (268 miles) road, 368km (228 miles) cross-country

This photograph gives a good impression of the hexagonal design of the T-34 turret.

T-34 variants

The robust T-34 chassis lent itself well as a base for other fighting vehicles. The first was the Su-122 self-propelled gun (SPG), which entered production in December 1942 at Sverdlovsk and mounted the M-30S 122mm howitzer Model 1931/37. The Su-122 was deployed early in 1943 and 1,148 units were produced before production ceased in 1944. The second SPG was the Su-85, which was armed with the D-5S Model 1943 gun. A dedicated tank destroyer, the Su-85 was a very effective weapon and 2,050 examples were built before it was phased out in favour of the more powerful Su-100, which carried the D-10S 100mm gun. By the end of the war 1,800 had been produced. Production continued for some time after the war and was resumed in Czechoslovakia in the 1950s, many of the Czech examples being exported. One version of the T-34, the PT-34, was converted to the mine-clearance role, fitted with minerollers extending in front of the vehicle, and others were applied to combat engineering and battlefield recovery tasks. The OT-34 was a flame-throwing variant with an internally-mounted flamethrower replacing the hull machine gun.

The German Army's T-34s

Many T-34s were captured by the Germans in the fighting on the Eastern Front, and carried the Wehrmacht designation T-34 747(r). Damaged vehicles were mostly repaired in workshops at Riga and their equipment modified to German standards by the addition of a radio and other internal equipment. The first captured T-34s entered German service during the summer of 1941. In order to prevent recognition mistakes, large-dimension crosses or even swastikas were painted on the tanks, including on top of the turret, in order to reduce the risk of attack by friendly aircraft. Modified T-34s were also used as artillery tractors, recovery vehicles, and ammunition carriers. Badly damaged tanks were either dug in as pillboxes or were used for testing and training purposes.

Captured T-34s pressed into service with the Wehrmacht carried a profusion of identification markings. These images show a Model 1941 and Model 1942. Note the twin hatches on the latter. (Courtesy of Anthony Tucker-Jones)

The introduction of the F-34 gun gave the T-34's turret an entirely different profile. Note the altered shape of the gun mantle. (Tom Cooper)

A T-34 gives protection to a squad of Soviet infantry.

Production of the early-model T-34 revealed some snags which had to be addressed before mass production could really get under way. One of the most serious involved the armour plating, which was of poor quality and had to be replaced. The L-11 gun selected as the T-34's main armament also failed to live up to expectations and a much better weapon, the F-34 designed by a team in Gorki, was proposed, but no one was prepared to authorize a change and the first series-produced T-34s were fitted with the L-11. (Tom Cooper)

This camouflaged T-34 Model 1940, armed with the L-11 gun, bears the popular slogan 'Za Stalina' (For Stalin). The tank has a cast turret. On these early machines, even the front idler wheel was rubber-rimmed. (Tom Cooper)

Front view of a T-34/76, showing driver's hatch and hull-mounted machine gun.

T-34 Model 1941 of the Independent Tank Brigade, autumn 1941, with F-34 main gun. The F-34 had a higher muzzle velocity than the earlier F-11, giving its projectiles a much better penetrating power. The slogan on the turret reads 'Crush the Fascists'. It was during the Spanish Civil War that the two extreme ideologies of Fascism and Communism first clashed head-on, and it became fashionable to paint patriotic slogans on armoured vehicles. (Tom Cooper)

The legend Gorkovskii Pioner on the turret of this T-34 Model 1941 honours the fund-raising contribution of the 'Pioneer' youth organizations in the Gorky region, who raised 250,000 roubles for the tank's construction at the Gorky plant. In all, seven tanks were built during the war with money raised by the Pioneers. (Tom Cooper)

T-34 Model 1941 with welded turret. (Source unknown)

The T-34s shown here are wearing the olive drab camouflage applied as standard to all T-34s before delivery to front-line units. There were no standard variations in this basic camouflage scheme, although tanks of a few units were camouflaged with a reddish brown pattern on the dark green background. In winter, many tanks were sprayed with white paint or lime over the original dark green, which still showed through the additional material. (Tom Cooper)

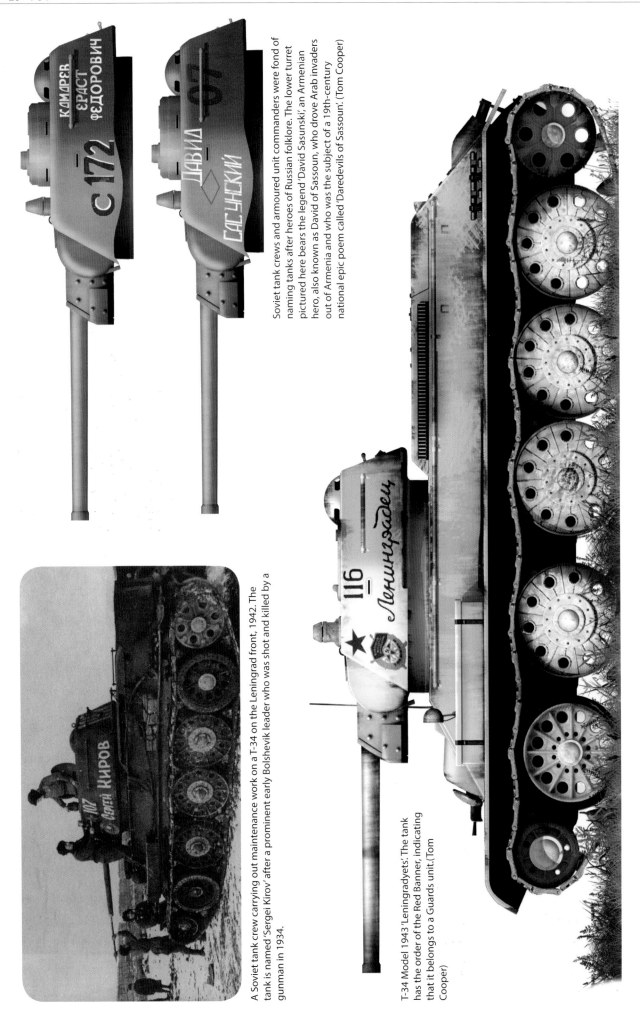

A Soviet tank crew carrying out maintenance work on a T-34 on the Leningrad front, 1942. The tank is named 'Sergei Kirov' after a prominent early Bolshevik leader who was shot and killed by a gunman in 1934.

Soviet tank crews and armoured unit commanders were fond of naming tanks after heroes of Russian folklore. The lower turret pictured here bears the legend 'David Sasunski', an Armenian hero, also known as David of Sassoun, who drove Arab invaders out of Armenia and who was the subject of a 19th-century national epic poem called 'Daredevils of Sassoun'. (Tom Cooper)

T-34 Model 1943 'Leningradyets'. The tank has the order of the Red Banner, indicating that it belongs to a Guards unit.(Tom Cooper)

Tactical insignia applied on turrets of T-34/85 tanks of the 2nd Guards Tank Army 1944–1945. From left: IX Guards Tanks Corps, XII Guards Tanks Corps and I Mechanized Corps. (Tom Cooper)

The most common tactical marking, as seen on this T-34 before the number 14, was a rhomboid, the upper half containing the battalion letter and the lower half with the individual vehicle number. (Tom Cooper)

This T-34 Model 1943, bearing the slogan 'First to Berlin', now features a commander's cupola. (Tom Cooper)

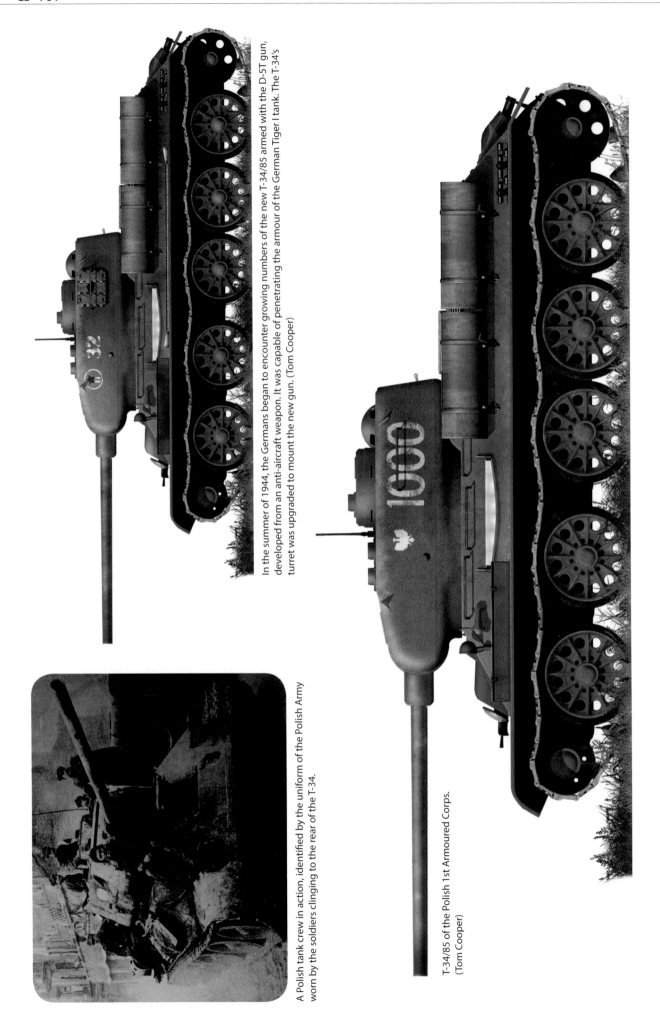

In the summer of 1944, the Germans began to encounter growing numbers of the new T-34/85 armed with the D-5T gun, developed from an anti-aircraft weapon. It was capable of penetrating the armour of the German Tiger I tank. The T-34's turret was upgraded to mount the new gun. (Tom Cooper)

A Polish tank crew in action, identified by the uniform of the Polish Army worn by the soldiers clinging to the rear of the T-34.

T-34/85 of the Polish 1st Armoured Corps. (Tom Cooper)

Turret artwork: The slogan "Dzerzhinskii" on the camouflaged turret of this T-34 Model 1941, not only commemorates Lenin's notorious secret police chief, but also indicates that the vehicle was produced by the Dzerzhinskii tank factory, a division of the Stalin Ural Tank Factory 183. (Tom Cooper)

Защитник *Ленинградец* **МОСКВА**

ЛЕНИНГРАДА **Комсомолец**

300 448 116 ДМИТРИЙ ДОНСКОЙ

In 1943, the Russian Orthodox Church raised over eight million roubles to finance the production of a new tank battalion. In February 1944, the Patriarch Sergius presented the Soviet Army with an independent T-34 flamethrower battalion named after the Russian hero Dmitri Donskoi (Dmitry of the Don), a 14th-century prince of Moscow who defeated the Tatars in the Battle of Kulikova. It was one of the first units equipped with the new T-34/85 Model 1943 tanks, and also the OT-34 flamethrower version.

T-34/85 Model 1943 of the Dmitry Donskoy Battalion, a unit raised thanks to donations by the Russian Orthodox Church. (Tom Cooper)

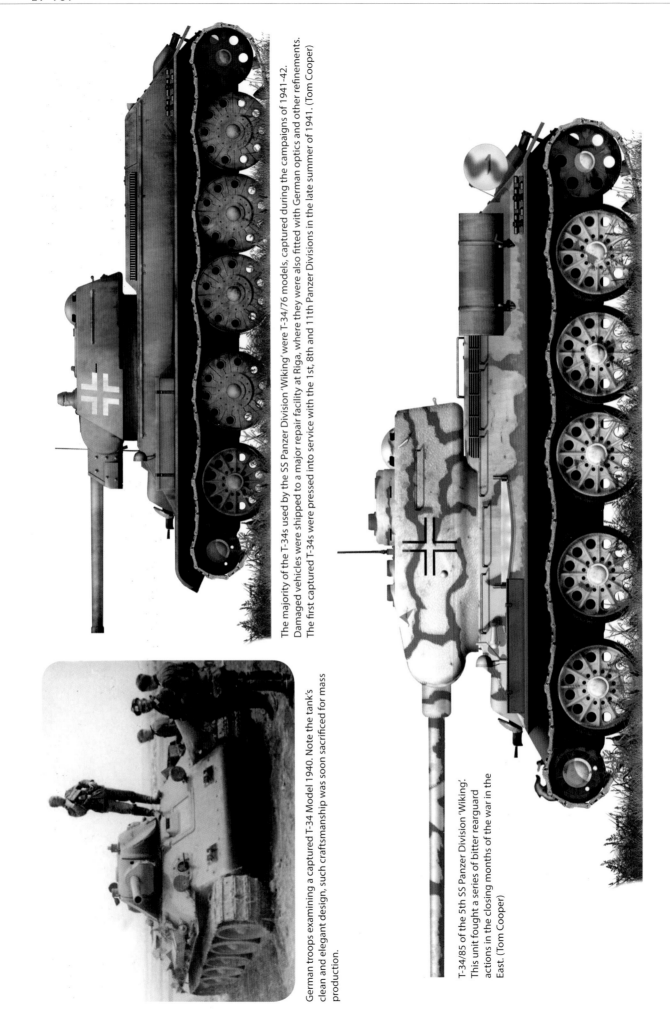

The majority of the T-34s used by the SS Panzer Division 'Wiking' were T-34/76 models, captured during the campaigns of 1941–42. Damaged vehicles were shipped to a major repair facility at Riga, where they were also fitted with German optics and other refinements. The first captured T-34s were pressed into service with the 1st, 8th and 11th Panzer Divisions in the late summer of 1941. (Tom Cooper)

German troops examining a captured T-34 Model 1940. Note the tank's clean and elegant design, such craftsmanship was soon sacrificed for mass production.

T-34/85 of the 5th SS Panzer Division 'Wiking'. This unit fought a series of bitter rearguard actions in the closing months of the war in the East. (Tom Cooper)

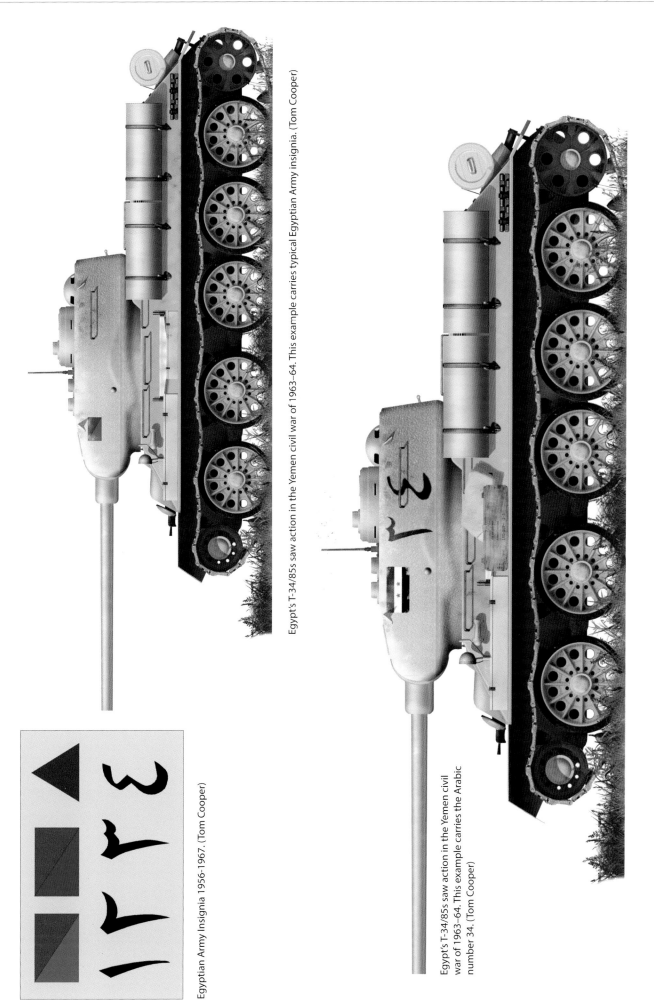

Egypt's T-34/85s saw action in the Yemen civil war of 1963–64. This example carries typical Egyptian Army insignia. (Tom Cooper)

Egyptian Army Insignia 1956-1967. (Tom Cooper)

Egypt's T-34/85s saw action in the Yemen civil war of 1963–64. This example carries the Arabic number 34. (Tom Cooper)

T-34/76
1942
1:16 Scale
Brian Richardson

This is one of four T-34 kits in 1/16 scale marketed by Trumpeter starting in 2004. Their T34/76 Model 1942 kit contains 764 styrene parts, 20 rubber tyres, 10 steel springs, two PE frets, copper tow cable, a 20-page instruction book and a small decal sheet with one option. I chose to modify the basic kit to represent a Krasnoye Sormovo Zadov 112 tank with features characteristic to this factory. From reference sources some of these features were a step-welded glacis, a relocated headlight, hand rails, turret ring splash guard, a PTK-5 periscope and a hooded tail light. At the time of this build there wasn't much in after-market product available and I prefer to scratch build anyway, so it was out with the styrene sheet, wire, putty and lots of references. The engine cover is mould solid with the upper hull and not much of the engine is visible through the smaller central hatch cover so a little surgery and some card made this removable. The other major job was to replace the wheel nuts, there are only eight and should be 10 to each wheel. I ground these off and replaced them with Meng product spaced out with a homemade paper template. The model was finished in Tamiya acrylics, oil washes and a variety of pastel chalks.

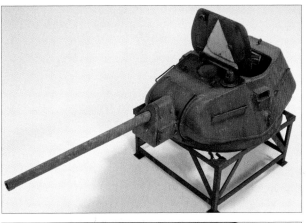

T-34/76

BERLIN 1945

1:35 Scale
Philipp Gross

The model is the ICM kit 35365 with old-style Dragon tracks, a turned barrel by RB Model and some leftover Dragon photoetched parts. It was painted with Tamiya colours, the main shade is XF-67 Nato Green. The weathering was done with generic artist's oils and pigments.

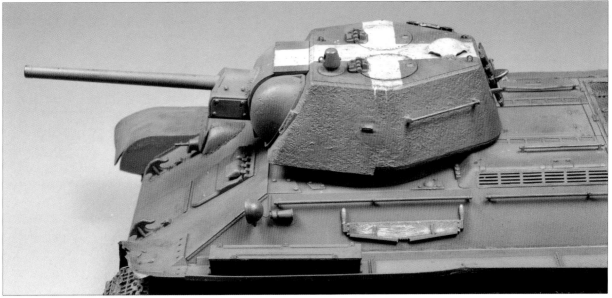

T-34/76
1941
1:35 Scale
Gary Riley

This is the Dragon T-34/76 in 1/35th scale. It was built out of the box. It was painted with Ammo by Mig acrylic paints and weathered with Mig Ammo filters. It was the first time I used filters on a model. I also used Vallejo pigments and washes. In all the build went well and I enjoyed it.

T-34/85
1943 'DAVID SASUNSKI'
1:35 Scale
Byeol Han

This is the Dragon Factory no.112 T-34/76 (kit #6584) converted to an earlier version with a DEF Model D-5T Early Version turret. The tracks are invididual track-links from AFV Club. The figures are from Hobby Fan.

The range of T-34 kits to various scales is so diverse that modellers have the opportunity to combine components from two or more to produce their own variations of chosen models, adding and refining pieces to make their chosen variant more realistic. This particularly applies to decals, which sometimes left a lot to be desired in the earlier kits.

One aspect that makes the T-34 attractive to modellers is the wide variety of camouflage schemes applied to the tank. In general, the standard paintwork applied to Soviet tanks was dark green paint overall. Tanks of a few units were camouflaged with a reddish brown pattern on the dark green background. In winter, many tanks wore camouflage of white paint or lime over the original dark green, which still showed through the additional material. The names of significant people, cities or patriotic slogans were often applied to the vehicle turrets.

This T-34/85 with Spaced Mesh Armour by Dave Willaims is his showcase attempt at reproducing Adam Wilder's brilliant T-34/85. Dave used the AFV Club T-34/85 with full interior along with Aber fenders, fuel tanks and mesh screens. His one criticism regards the kit's one-piece tracks, so he bought some AM resin workable ones and was happier with the outcome.

This 1/35th scale T-34/85, depicting a Model 1944 produced by Factory 174, is a recent offering from AFV Club, a manufacturer of kits and accessories established in the Republic of China in the late 1980s. AFV Club specializes in military vehicles, although it has also reissued some aircraft kits originating with other manufacturers. One of the interesting things about this model is that the turret and upper hull are finished in clear plastic, showing the vehicle's internal equipment, rather like a cutaway drawing. The modeller has the option of displaying the vehicle in this manner, or applying paint to end up with a very realistic T-34/85 Model 1944. Construction of the kit is straightforward, with very detailed instructions guiding the modeller through thirty separate stages of the assembly, starting with the lower hull and wheels. There are also precise instructions on the paint to use on individual items, and three decal options are included, with instructions on how to apply them. Six steps are devoted to building the interior of the hull, complete with machine gun and 85mm main gun ammunition, pedal linkages and a floor escape hatch.

Reviewers of this kit are enthusiastic about the standard of accuracy, with particular regard to the V2 engine and transmission assembly. This takes up two pages of the instruction manual, and items like the flywheel/cooling fan assembly are completed in quite amazing detail. The engine compartment features a separate access hatch and cooling slats.

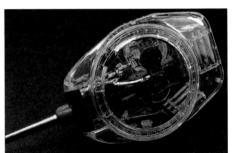

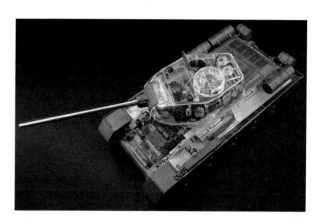

One of the most popular large-scale T-34 examples, on the market for many years now, is Tamiya's 1/35th scale T-34, available in both T-34/76 and T-34/85 variants. The latter is possibly the more detailed, with accurate representations of the sloped hull armour and the rough cast-iron finish which was a feature of 'no-frills' Russian tanks. The weld joints are also accurate. The long-barrelled 85mm main gun is removable, and the commander's and gunner's hatches can be opened. The model has a choice of decals, representing the markings of four Soviet tanks and one North Korean. Tamiya has also produced a 1/25th scale T-34/85 in limited edition.

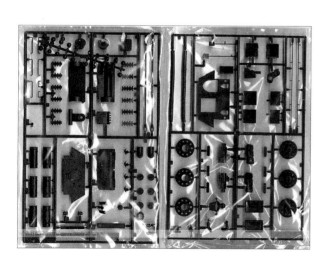

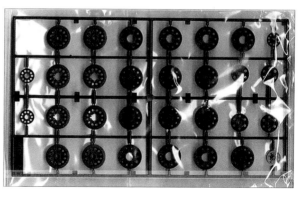

One of the more recent releases, in 2015, was a 1/35th scale T-34/85 offered by the Korean plastic model company Academy, representing a vehicle built by Factory No. 112. The kit is moulded in dark green styrene on 16-part sprues, plus two trees moulded in grey styrene for the track components, and one fret of photo-etched parts for the rear intake cover. The kit includes decals for two Soviet and three North Korean T-34s. It also provides a choice of two turrets, allowing you to choose between an early 1944 variant or a later 1944–1945 version.

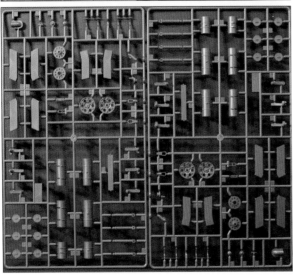

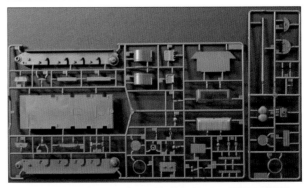

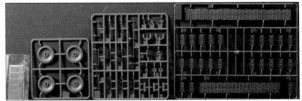

Maquette's offering of an early-model 1/35th T-34/85 has received mixed reviews, although generally it is described as an interesting and accurate kit of a highly significant version of the T-34, and the inclusion of a resin turret makes the package more attractive at a reasonable price. The kit accurately depicts the specific features of the Model 1943 including the forward-mounted turret cupola, rounded fenders, alternately located fuel drums and looped turret-lifting hooks. The kit otherwise shares many major parts with the T-34/85 Model 1945 variant released earlier by Maquette, such as the lower and upper hull, suspension, running gear etc. These parts, although accurate, do suffer from sink marks and quite a lot of flash. Modellers are always on the lookout for this; on injection-moulded kits sometimes the two halves of the mould do not meet perfectly and some molten plastic can squeeze out in between the moulds. The result is parts that have a thin flap of plastic

all around the edge where the seam is. This rarely happens on recently released kits that are produced with new moulds.

For the modeller who prefers to tackle a large-scale subject, the biggest (and most expensive) is the 1/16th scale T-34 by the Chinese company Trumpeter. It has received mixed reviews, although it provides plenty of scope for adaptation.

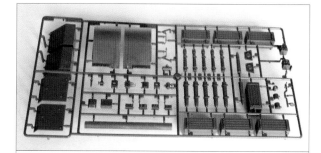

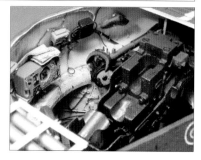

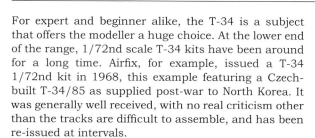

For expert and beginner alike, the T-34 is a subject that offers the modeller a huge choice. At the lower end of the range, 1/72nd scale T-34 kits have been around for a long time. Airfix, for example, issued a T-34 1/72nd kit in 1968, this example featuring a Czech-built T-34/85 as supplied post-war to North Korea. It was generally well received, with no real criticism other than the tracks are difficult to assemble, and has been re-issued at intervals.

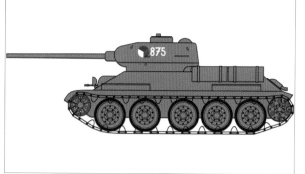

Another supplier of large-scale T-34 kits is the whole-sale distributor Dragon Models Ltd (DML), which offers both the T-34/76 and T-34/85 in 1/35th scale. Dragon's T-34/76 Model 1942 1/72nd kit, which has been around now for a number of years, also comes highly recommended. It contains 92 styrene parts and four pages of easy-to-follow line drawing instructions, together with five decal marking schemes.

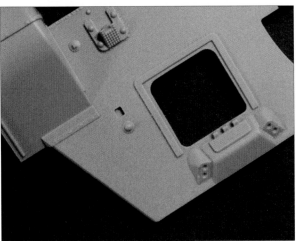

The Russian company Zvezda's 1/35th T-34 Model 1941/42 has had favourable reviews and is simple to assemble. The kit was originally released in 1997.

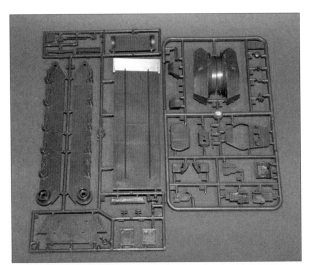

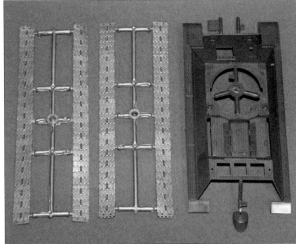

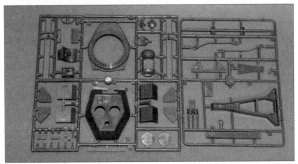

The opposition: the German Panzers

Numerically, the most important German medium tank at the start of the invasion was the Panzerkampfwagen PzKpfw III, popularly known as the Panzer III. Its development was the result of a German Army requirement, issued in the mid-1930s, that each armoured battalion should be equipped with three companies of relatively light medium tanks and one company of heavier and more powerful support tanks, the latter emerging as the Panzer Mk IV. Whereas the Panzer II was designed for the infantry support role, the Mk III was intended to fight and destroy other tanks. Mass production of the tank began in 1939. By mid-1941 it was armed with a 50mm main gun that was effective against all Soviet tanks except the T-34.

The other medium tank, the Panzer IV, was to become the workhorse of the German Panzer divisions in the Second World War, operating in many different roles. It was armed with the short 75mm KwK L/24 low-velocity gun, which fired a high-explosive round and was effective against fortifications and infantry, but which lacked accuracy. In 1941, following the first encounters between the Panzer IV and the T-34, the Panzer IV Ausführung F was equipped with a redesigned turret mounting a more powerful 75mm L/43 anti-tank gun. In this guise it became the Panzer IVF2, later renamed the Panzer IVG. This variant remained basically unchanged except for upgrades in its main armament and armour, dictated by operational experience. These upgrades, particularly in gunnery and optical sighting systems, enabled the Panzer IV to hold its own with the T-34.

The driving force behind the development of Germany's new medium tanks – restricted to these two types by economic constraints – was Colonel (later General) Heinz Guderian, whose plan was to concentrate these armoured fighting vehicles in formations, the celebrated Panzer divisions, instead of splitting them up in packages between the various field armies. It was a formula that worked with devastating effect.

The Wehrmacht's armoured divisions, and those of Germany's allies on the Eastern Front, also used considerable numbers of a Czech-designed medium tank, the LT-38, later redesignated Panzer 38(t). Originally armed with a 37mm gun, later upgraded to 47mm, it was no match

An immaculate Panzer III Ausführung H on display at France's Musée des Blindés, Saumur. The Panzer III was used by all Germany's allies on the Eastern Front.

General Heinz Guderian. (Bundesarchiv)

for the T-34 and suffered heavy losses from the beginning of the invasion.

During the first five months of 1941, although production of the T-34 and the heavier KV-1 was starting to accelerate, it was still far too slow to bring the replacement programme envisaged by the Soviet high command to anywhere near the desired level. Crews found it difficult to make the transition from the earlier T-26 and BT-7 tanks, so that training was slow, and many Soviet tank men would go to war with little more than 72 hours of classroom instruction and only a very basic acquaintance with the T-34 and its systems.

As a result, the bulk of the 19,000 tanks that equipped the Soviet mechanized formations at the beginning of June 1941 were still T-26s and BTs. Total production

The Panzer IV was a match for the T-34, but was almost always outnumbered in action against the Soviet tank. (Courtesy of Anthony Tucker-Jones)

Centre: A T-34 Model 1941 pictured at the Kubinka Tank Museum. The drab green plain scheme was universally applied to all T-34s.

Above: A T-34 and its crew preparing for action. (Source unknown, via J.R. Cavanagh)

Poor leadership, inadequate training, faulty intelligence, non-existent communications and mechanical problems all combined to spread chaos within the Soviet armoured formations from the very beginning. Because Soviet tank crews were not trained to carry out mechanical repairs in the field, hundreds of tanks broke down and were abandoned before getting anywhere near the battle area. The lack of radio sets meant that individual tank commanders could not communicate with one another, nor could they contact the support vehicles bringing up ammunition and fuel. The situation was well expressed by General Ryabishev, writing of events that unfolded on 25 June, three days after the German attack. Units of his VIII Corps deployed to the northwest of Brody that afternoon, having wandered around much of the front trying to co-ordinate a counter-attack with other armoured formations.

During the nearly 500-kilometre march, the Corps lost up to half of its older tanks and a substantial portion of its artillery and anti-tank guns to both enemy air attack and mechanical breakdowns. All of the tanks still in service also required varying degrees of maintenance work and were not capable of operating over long distances. Thus, even before the start of the counteroffensive the Corps found itself in a drastically weakened state.

Nevertheless, VIII Corps met with some initial success when it engaged units of the 11th Panzer Division on 26 June, its T-34s and KV-1s punching a hole through hastily prepared enemy defences. German anti-tank gunners found to their consternation that their 37mm rounds bounced off the armour of the modern Soviet tanks; in one instance, elsewhere on the front, a lone T-34 penetrated nine miles inside the enemy lines before it was destroyed by a shot from a 100mm gun, fired from astern. The 37mm Pak (Panzerabwehrkanone) 36 was the Wehrmacht's main anti-tank weapon at

of the T-34 and KV-1 at this point was 1,600 units, and of these 751 had been issued to three formations, the IV, VIII and XV Mechanized Corps, all in the Kiev Military District on the Southwestern Front. They were commanded, respectively, by Major General Andrey Vlasov, Lieutenant General Dmitry Ryabishev, and Major General Ignat Karpezo.

It was these formations, based between 60 and 180 miles from the start line of Operation Barbarossa that bore the brunt of the German invasion of 22 June 1941. Their poorly conducted counterattacks would encounter formidable opposition in the shape of General Ewald von Kleist's First Panzer Group, which had the task of driving a wedge between the Soviet Fifth and Sixth armies and driving on to Kiev.

the start of Operation Barbarossa; a newer weapon, the 50mm Pak 38, had just begun to enter service in small numbers, but only two of these guns were available per infantry regiment. The German anti-tank gunners could at best attempt to immobilize the T-34s and KVs by firing at their tracks, allowing infantry to close in and attempt to blow them up with shaped charges. Immobilized tanks were also vulnerable to field artillery fire, and especially vulnerable to the formidable 88mm anti-aircraft gun, which had already proved it worth in the anti-tank role in other campaigns, but the fifty-one battalions armed with the 88mm were generally assigned to army and corps headquarters.

Much of VIII Corps' success was achieved by Brigade Commissar Popel, who assembled a strike force from units of the 34th Tank Division, which had not yet been committed to combat. Popel's group had about 300 tanks, including 100 T-34s and KV-1s. It surprised and defeated the rear of 11th Panzer Division and captured the strategic road junction at Brody, as well as cutting off 11th Panzer's supply lines. However, an attempt by Ryabishev to exploit this success with his 303 remaining tanks, including forty-nine T-34s and forty-six KVs, ended in failure and he was forced to retreat, having lost eighteen T-34s and three KV-1s. By 7 July 1941 VIII Corps' effective strength had been reduced to forty-three tanks of all types, a mere five per cent of its pre-invasion number.

The retreat of VIII Corps was covered by Andrei Vlasov's IV Corps, the strongest armoured force in the Ukraine, with 313 T-34s and 101 KV-1s. It responded late to the German threat and its assets were never assembled in sufficient strength to mount a serious counterattack. Nevertheless, by 12 July it was reduced to six per cent of its KV tanks, twelve per cent of its T-34s and four per cent of its older BTs.

One of the biggest Soviet successes in this phase was registered by the 10th Tank Division of XV Mechanized Corps, which destroyed twenty of 11th Panzer Division's tanks on 23 June for the loss of six T-34s and twenty BTs. Shortage of ammunition then compelled it to withdraw, but it launched a determined counterattack on 26 June, destroying twenty-three German tanks and an infantry battalion at Radikhev. Its own losses were thirteen KV and twelve BT-7s.

The four-day battle between First Panzer Group and the Soviet Mechanized Corps, known variously as the Battle of Brody and the Battle of Dubno, was the fiercest of the whole invasion phase of Barbarossa. It cost the Germans 200 tanks and the Russians 800. Apart from the numerical losses, the difference was that the Germans were able to fight on; the Russians were not. The VIII Mechanized Corps was so badly depleted that it was disbanded by the Stavka, its surviving units being distributed among other Soviet formations. A key factor in the German success was the Luftwaffe's overwhelming air superiority, some 200 Russian tanks being knocked out by low-level air strikes during the battle. A similar fate befell IV Mechanized Corps in August, when it was almost totally destroyed at the Battle of Uman, as First Panzer Group drove on towards Kiev.

In the early phase of Operation Barbarossa the Russians lost hundreds of T-34s, not always as the result of enemy action. (Courtesy of Anthony Tucker-Jones)

The smouldering wreck of a T-34, destroyed by a German self-propelled gun. (Bundesarchiv)

Top: A German soldier, wearing the confident smile of the victor, strolls past disabled and abandoned T-34s. (Bundesarchiv)

Above: Soviet tanks of the 19th Division destroyed during the Battle of Brody. These are all elderly T-26s. (Source unknown, via J.R. Cavanagh)

Right: General Andrei Vlasov. He later changed sides and fought for the Germans, then changed sides again towards the end of the war. He was tried and hanged by the Russians. (Bundesarchiv)

The massive inroads into Soviet territory following the German offensive forced the Soviet government to undertake the wholesale evacuation of key armaments factories from western Russia to the east of the Ural mountains. Under the personal supervision of Alexander Morozov, all skilled engineers and labourers, machinery and stock were evacuated from the Kharkov factory to Nizhny Tagil, where they were relocated to the site of the Dzherzhinski Ural Railcar Factory. The new establishment was renamed Stalin Ural Tank Factory No.

183. At the same time, the Kirov Factory was evacuated from Leningrad only weeks before the city was surrounded by the enemy and co-located, together with the Kharkov Diesel Factory, at the Stalin Tractor Factory in Chelyabinsk. Workers and machinery from Leningrad's Voroshilov Tank Factory No. 174 were incorporated into the Ural Factory and the new Factory No. 174 at Omsk. Smaller factories and machine shops under threat, and able to be evacuated in time, were absorbed by the Ordzhonikidze Heavy Machine Tool Works.

The problems faced by the German tanks as the initial phase of Operation Barbarossa drew to a close were summed up by General Gunther Blumentritt, Chief of Staff of the Fourth Army, which was part of Army Group Centre:

It was appallingly difficult country for tank movement – great virgin forests, widespread swamps, terrible roads, and bridges not strong enough to bear the weight of tanks ... Such country was bad enough for the tanks, but worse still for the transport accompanying them – carrying their fuel, their supplies, and all the auxiliary troops they needed. Nearly all this transport consisted of wheeled vehicles, which could not move off the roads, nor move on it if the sand turned into mud. An hour or two of rain reduced the Panzer forces to stagnation. It was an extraordinary sight, with groups of them strung out over a hundred miles stretch, all stuck – until the sun came out and the ground dried.

And rain it did, consistently, beginning in September, with conditions becoming increasingly less favourable to the Panzers and more favourable to the Soviet armour, with its better cross-country manoeuvrability. However, the enforced move of the factories had slowed tank production to little more than a trickle, and new-build T-34s had to be deployed in small packages to units all along the front, reinforcing those that had escaped the German onslaught.

In October 1941, while von Kleist's First Panzer Group drove on to Kiev, Army Group Centre, General Heinz Guderian's Second Panzer Group thrust directly for Moscow. On 3 October its spearhead, 4th Panzer Division under General Freiherr von Langermann, captured Orel, just over 100 miles from the Soviet capital. Despite being short of fuel, Langermann pushed on through open country.

Between the Panzers and the Moscow defensive perimeter lay a single force of tanks, about fifty T-34s of the 4th Tank Brigade, subordinate to I Guards Rifle Corps, under Colonel Mikhail Katukov, commander of the Soviet Tank School at Kharkov. Katukov was fortunate in that he could draw on some of the most able and experienced tank crews in the Red Army, and now he used them to good effect. On 6 October, his T-34s encountered the advance echelons of 4th Panzer near Tula. While units of the Rifle Corps made frontal assaults on the advancing Germans, the T-34s attacked the flanks of 4th Panzer and destroyed more than thirty Panzer IVs, whose short 75mm guns were ineffective unless they were able to engage a T-34 from astern and secure a hit in the Soviet tank's vulnerable engine compartment. The T-34s, taking advantage of their ability to manoeuvre through terrain that was impassable to the Panzers, were able to conceal themselves in the woods that flanked the Germans' axis of advance and pick off the enemy tanks one by one. In honour of its achievement at Tula, the 4th Tank Brigade was given the title of the 1st Guards Tank Brigade, the first to be so honoured.

On the following day, the smoke from the tanks that still smouldered on the battlefield mingled with the first snow of the Russian winter, which quickly melted and turned the roads and open country into a quagmire. Then came the big freeze, which enabled the Panzers to resume their advance over the frozen terrain; but from 6 December a major Soviet counteroffensive relieved the pressure on Moscow. The success of this offensive was due at least in part to the deployment of British Valentine and Matilda tanks to the front, providing much-needed support for the still understrength Soviet armoured divisions, a fact ignored by Soviet historians for decades after the war.

The first twenty Vickers Mk III Valentine medium tanks were shipped to the Soviet Union via the northern port of Archangel in October 1941 and were sent to the tank training school at Kazan. They were quickly followed by 120 more, reaching the front in November. According to German sources, the first contact between the Panzers and British tanks occurred on 26 November 1941, twenty-one Valentines were assigned to the 138th Independent Tank Battalion, which was in action against German forces near the Volga Reservoir to the north of Moscow. Other Soviet armoured units using British tanks in the defence of Moscow during this period were the 136th Independent Tank Battalion, the 131st Independent Tank Brigade, and the 146th Tank Brigade.

Both the Valentine and Matilda – which was used only in very small numbers from late December in the battle for Moscow – had good armour protection but were under-gunned, being armed with only a 40mm two-pounder main gun. Though they were inferior to the KV-1 and T-34 in every aspect, their cross-country performance in poor conditions was comparable to that of the BT-7 and they performed a valuable second-line defence role. Deliveries of both British tanks continued through the spring and summer of 1942; most of the

Valentines were built in Canada, which shipped 1,420 to the USSR.

Meanwhile, T-34 production continued, the workers of the factories newly established in the east making superhuman efforts under often appalling conditions throughout the Siberian winter. Their efforts were desperately needed; of the 2,800 T-34s produced in 1940–41, 2,300 had been lost.

Above: T-34 production in full swing at the Stalin Ural Tank Factory No. 183. The relocation of Russia's tank production facilities was little short of miraculous. (Novosti)

Left: General Ewald von Kleist. (Bundesarchiv)

Victim of a T-34: a knocked-out Panzer IV. (Source unknown, via J.R. Cavanagh)

Top: The British
Valentine tank, seen
here in the Kubinka
Tank Museum, was at
the forefront of Allied
Lend-Lease shipments
to the USSR. Most of
those supplied were
manufactured in
Canada.

Above: T-34s carrying
Soviet reinforcements
to battle in Stalingrad.
(TASS)

Although it drove three deep wedges into enemy-held territory, the Soviet Winter Offensive of 1942 failed in its primary aim. Notwithstanding desperate Soviet assaults, fortified centres of German resistance held out until the spring thaw, by which time both sides had virtually fought themselves to a standstill. Yet there was to be little respite. The Soviet high command was already planning another major counteroffensive, while the Germans were getting ready for a massive thrust to the Don and the Volga and into the Caucasus, which – in addition to the vast wealth of the region's oilfields – would give them possible access to the Middle East by the northern route. For their projected offensive, the Germans had assembled seventy-four divisions between Voronezh and the Crimea.

The Germans struck first, on 8 May 1942, the first blows falling on the Soviet Crimean front. The attack smashed through the Soviet Forty-fourth Army and thrust on towards the Sea of Azov. Faulty intelligence had led the Russians to believe the offensive would not begin in this sector, and consequently they were not prepared to meet it. The Soviet Fifty-first Army was surrounded by General Erich von Manstein's Eleventh Army, and Kerch captured, the Russians being forced to evacuate the Kerch Peninsula. The last Soviet bastion in the Crimea, Sevastopol, bombarded from both air and land, held out for twenty-five days before its evacuation was also ordered on 30 June.

Meanwhile, to the north, Soviet troops of the Southwestern Front under Marshal Timoshenko had launched a limited offensive with Kharkov as its objective, and had temporarily driven a wedge through the German Sixth Army to the north and south of the town, but the offensive lacked adequate air support and in mid-May the Soviet Sixth and Thirty-eighth armies were driven back to the Donets river by a strong German counterattack, supported by von

In mid-January 1942, the Russians – encouraged by their successful defence of Moscow, and with their front-line forces reinforced by fresh divisions from Siberia – launched a major offensive on the Kalinin front with the aim of encircling Army Group Centre. In bitter cold and deep snow, the Third and Fourth Soviet Shock armies, driving through the Valday Hills to the north of Rzhev, hammered a wedge between the German Army Group North and Army Group Centre on the Western Front, the Russians advanced along the Smolensk highway and recaptured Mozhaisk. In the south, the Soviet Thirty-third Army launched a strong thrust towards Vyazma.

By the beginning of
1942 more German
anti-tank units were
armed with the
formidable 88mm gun,
converted from its
original anti-tank role.
(Bundesarchiv)

Kleist's First Panzer Army. This thrust effectively sealed the fate of the major part of five Soviet armies, which became isolated by von Kleist's Panzers when Marshal Timoshenko withdrew to form a defensive line on the Donets. Though some units did manage to fight their way out of the trap, the greater part of the encircled armies had to surrender. It was the biggest haul of prisoners the Germans had taken since the war in the east began.

The stage was now set for the massive German offensive that would take them through the eastern Ukraine to the Volga. In readiness for this, Field Marshal Fedor von Bock's Army Group South was reinforced until, at the end of June 1942, it comprised ninety divisions, ten of them armoured. In an attempt to prepare for the coming attack, the Russians reorganized their forces in the southwest into four fronts: the Bryansk Front, the Southwestern Front, the Southern Front and the North Caucasus Front. While this reorganization went on, the Soviet high command brought in reinforcements transferred from the east, and these helped to check the German advance towards the end of July.

The Soviet armoured forces were also showing signs of recovery; at the beginning of July some 13,500 tanks were in service, about sixteen per cent supplied by Britain and the United States, in equal quantities.

The increase in Soviet tank production encouraged the Stavka to authorize the formation of a new type of tank corps, each comprising three tank brigades and one mechanized brigade, with an establishment of twenty KVs, forty T-34s and forty light tanks. Later, the strength of a tank corps was increased to 168 tanks, the majority of which were T-34s. The tank corps was intended to operate in conjunction with another new formation, the mechanized corps. About the same size as a Panzer division, the mechanized corps consisted of three brigades: one armoured, one infantry

and one artillery. Its task was to exploit any breakthrough made by the tank corps.

Another innovation was the tank army, based on two tank corps and a rifle division. The tank army was potentially a very powerful formation, but suffered heavy losses when first deployed in May 1942, mainly because of poor tactics and mechanical issues.

In mid-1942 the Germans received reinforcements from Army Group A and the Voronezh sector, and this fresh blood enabled them to drive a wedge through the Russian lines and reach the bend in the Don directly opposite Stalingrad. On the last day of July a new threat materialized in the shape of a thrust from the Caucasus front by the German Fourth Panzer Army, driving towards Stalingrad from the southwest. A week later, the German Sixth Army crossed the Don and established a foothold on the river's east bank. The battle for Stalingrad was on.

By the middle of September the Germans were in Stalingrad itself, their advance through the city bitterly contested by General Vasily Chuikov's Sixty-second Army. The Russians fought savagely, and every shattered building or stone wall that

Top: Soviet troops riding T-34s into battle during the fighting in the Crimea, May 1942. (Courtesy of Anthony Tucker-Jones)

Above: General Friedrich Paulus, commander of the German Sixth Army, pictured in southern Russia in January 1942. (Bundesarchiv)

Old and new: a horse-drawn sledge with supplies advancing towards Stalingrad alongside a T-34. (Courtesy of Anthony Tucker-Jones)

A T-34 churns up snow as it advances through Stalingrad at speed. It bears the legend 'Rodina' ('Motherland'). (Courtesy of Anthony Tucker-Jones)

A column of T-34s in Stalingrad after the surrender of the German Sixth Army. (TASS)

was seized by the attackers was paid for with dozens of human lives. The battle for Stalingrad became a guerrilla campaign, with individuals or small groups of soldiers stalking one another in the ruins and victory going to the fastest and the stealthiest.

Effective air support in the forward areas became impossible on both sides, with the front lines – where they existed – separated by a strip of land only a grenade-throw wide. Chuikov's forces, the decimated

remnants of his original six divisions, soon found themselves confined to a narrow sector along the west bank of the Volga, some eighteen miles long and no more than a mile and a half wide. The ferrying of reinforcements across the river was a hazardous business, as the crossing had to be made under heavy artillery fire and air attack. On 14 September, however, the 13th Guards Division under Lieutenant General Alexander Rodimtsev made the perilous trip and immediately went into action in the savage fighting for a hill known as Mamayev Kurgan, a vital objective. It dominated the river crossing, and whoever controlled it controlled Stalingrad. Twenty-four hours later, Rodimtsev's Guards had virtually ceased to exist – but they had held Mamayev Kurgan.

Towards the end of September, with the battle raging in the ruins of Stalingrad, the Soviet high command laid plans for a massive counteroffensive. Codenamed Operation Uranus, it would take the form of a giant pincer movement; one arm would strike northwestward from the south of the city, and the other would thrust southward from the middle Don area, the two linking up on the curve of the Don and nipping off the Stalingrad salient. In this salient were the German Fourth Panzer Army and Paulus's Sixth Army. The Soviet objective was to trap and destroy them both.

The Russians laid their plans carefully; the two arms of the pincer were to smash their way through the German defences at their weakest points, to the south of Stalingrad and near Serafimovitch, where Soviet forces already held a bridgehead on the south bank of the Don. In both these sectors, the Russians were opposed by troops of the Romanian Fourth Army which, as well as being inferior to the Russians in numbers of men and weapons, were for the most part poorly equipped.

The Soviet offensive in the southwest opened on the morning of 19 November in thick, freezing fog and snow, the assault preceded by a massive artillery barrage. Troops of the 126th and 302nd Rifle divisions of the Soviet Fifty-first Army, advancing on a three-mile front, were supported by the 55th and 158th Independent Tank regiments of IV Mechanized Corps, falling on the Romanian VI Corps, and against this onslaught the Romanian resistance rapidly crumbled, the Romanian troops beginning to surrender or flee as soon as the T-34s reached their forward positions. Within twenty-four hours the Soviet spearheads had advanced twenty miles into enemy territory; the retreat of the Romanian Fourth Army had become a rout, and it was only the intervention of the German 22nd Panzer Division, slowing the Russian advance, that prevented the annihilation of the Romanian forces.

Meanwhile, the offensive by the Stalingrad Front – which began at dawn on 20 November – had also broken through the enemy perimeter south of the city. The plan of attack had envisaged three armoured brigades advancing in parallel along three roads; instead, the whole force advanced along a single road, and the two brigades on the flank, the 36th and 59th, suffered heavy losses when they ran into minefields. Despite this setback the T-34s rolled on towards the town of Kalach, where the link-up with the armoured vanguard of the Southwestern Front was to take place. Kalach, with its strategic bridge over the Don, fell to General Rodin's XXVI Armoured Corps on the night of the 22nd, and the following afternoon the link-up was successfully achieved between the latter and IV Mechanized Corps.

For the 90,000 men trapped in the Stalingrad pocket, time was fast running out. Paulus, who had held on to the shattered city on the orders of the Fuhrer, with the latter's assurance that Sixth Army would not be abandoned, now had no choice: Sixth Army was no longer capable of breaking out of the trap without help from the outside. By 23 December any hope of breaking through the Soviet encirclement from outside had been abandoned, and in February 1943 Paulus surrendered the remnants of Sixth Army to the Russians.

Meanwhile, on 3 January 1943, with forces newly released from the Stalingrad fighting, the Soviet Caucasus Front had launched a major offensive aimed at wresting control of the Kuban peninsula from the Germans, who had been pouring troops and equipment into the area in readiness for their own offensive into the oil-rich Caucasus. The Kuban offensive ended on 14 February with the recapture of Rostov by the Russians, which effectively ended the threat to the Caucasus. Elsewhere, however, an attempt by the Soviet Southwestern and Voronezh fronts to encircle the German armies in the eastern Ukraine had failed, mainly because the Russian leaders believed that large quantities of enemy armour deployed to the area between the rivers Dnieper and Donets were there to cover the German retreat – and not to spearhead a German counterattack, as was actually the case.

The Russians took Kharkov on 16 February 1943 and raced on towards the strategic town of Dnepropetrovsk, and it was then that the Germans hit the offensive with everything they had. The Fourth Panzer Army attacked both flanks of the Southwestern Front and in a matter of days the Russians, battle-weary and badly over-extended, found themselves digging in along the line of the Don once more, back where they had started. The Germans recaptured Kharkov and Byelgorod, but the Russians quickly strengthened the Donets line and the enemy counteroffensive was halted.

With the coming of the spring thaw, large-scale operations along the whole front came to a standstill. As they had done a

year earlier, both sides took the opportunity to strengthen their forces in preparation for a summer offensive. The Germans knew that everything depended on the outcome of the summer of 1943. If they regained the initiative they would have a second chance to take Moscow; but if they lost it, the way would be open for a Soviet advance into central Europe.

The spring lull in the fighting had left the Soviet Central and Voronezh fronts in a potentially dangerous situation, with two German salient, at Orel and Kharkov, flanking a deep bulge to the west of Kursk. In this bulge the Russians had concentrated twelve armies, including two elite Guards and two tank armies. If the Germans could smash their way through the Russian defences to the north and south of Kursk

Top: A T-34 Model 1942 abandoned on a muddy road. (Bundeswehr)

Centre: This T-34 bears the sign 'Prisoner of War Camp' on its turret, with an arrow pointing the way. (Bundesarchiv)

Above: German Panzergrenadiers, in white camouflage clothing, inspect a wrecked T-34 in a Russian town. (Bundesarchiv)

Top: The 43-ton Panther tank, with frontal armour of 83mm thickness, a speed of 28mph and a main armament of one 75mm gun, was arguably the best medium tank of the Second World War. (Courtesy of Anthony Tucker-Jones)

Above: The Tiger I's main asset was its 88mm main gun, with 92 rounds of ammunition at its disposal. (Bundesarchiv)

Right: German Panzergrenadiers sheltering beside a T-34. The tank is fitted with an Uralmesh turret. (Source unknown)

they would split the Soviet front in two, cutting off all the Soviet forces within the Kursk salient and destroying them. If the German plan succeeded, the Red Army would have little hope of recovering from such a shattering defeat.

What followed, in the summer of 1943, was the largest tank battle in history, an epic struggle covering a vast area of the Russian steppe. It would be the decisive battle of the war on the eastern front, and its outcome would lead to the eventual collapse of the Wehrmacht in the east. It was also a battle in which the T-34 played a very prominent part.

Lack of space in this short work precludes describing the Battle of Kursk in detail, but some aspects are worthy of mention. First of all, the Russians were fully aware of the enemy's intentions, and had been for months. Field Marshal Erich von Manstein had wanted to launch the offensive against the Kursk salient at the end of April, when the ground had become sufficiently dry to permit unrestricted tank movement; but Hitler, worried by the destruction of Axis forces in North Africa and the possibility of an early Allied landing at some point in Western Europe, had convinced himself that the only way to ensure German victory in the east was to arm the Panzer divisions with the latest equipment, which in practice meant as many Tigers as could be spared, supported by the new Panzer V Panther medium tank and the Elefant self-propelled gun, neither of them yet tested in combat. In practice, the new fighting vehicles were mostly issued to the elite SS armoured divisions, the remainder still using the Panzer IV.

Hitler's prevarication created unacceptable delays and gave the Russians, armed with intelligence gleaned from numerous sources, time to prepare a formidable defence in depth, so strong that the German offensive would exhaust itself against it. During April, May and June 1943, using a 300,000-strong labour force, they established six separate belts of earthworks, each defended by huge concentrations of infantry, artillery and self-propelled guns, massed in and around strongpoints, to a depth of twenty-five miles. Mine defences were also formidable, 2,400 anti-tank and 2,700 anti-personnel mines being laid on every mile of front. Some 6,000 anti-tank guns were deployed in total. To the rear, and on the flanks of the static defences, masses of T-34 and KV tanks lay in wait, ready to confront any German breakthrough and launch a counterattack as soon as the enemy offensive showed signs of faltering.

Following a period of intensive air operations by both sides, the German offensive, codenamed Operation Citadel, was launched at dawn on 5 July 1943. Field Marshal Günther von Kluge's Army Group Centre attacked from the north flank of the bulge, with General Walther Model's Ninth Army leading. The plan was to drive toward Kursk and meet up with Field Marshal Erich von Manstein's Army Group South, General Hermann Hoth's Fourth Panzer Army and a formation known as Army Detachment Kempf, after its commander, General Werner Kempf.

Confronting the German forces were the Soviet Central Front, led by General Konstantin Rokossovsky, and the Voronezh Front, led by General Nikolai Vatutin. The Central Front, with the right wing reinforced by the Thirteenth and Seventeenth armies, was to defend the northern sector. To the south, the

Voronezh Front faced the German Army Group South with three armies and two in reserve. In this sector, from the start of the offensive, General Mikhail Katokov's First Tank Army, with over 650 tanks in the beginning, was in continual action against General Hoth's Fourth Panzer Army, and suffered horrendous losses; by 11 July, for example, First Tank Army's VI Tank Corps was reduced to about fifty tanks out of its original 200, and the army's other two tank corps were in no better shape. This left only the Fifth Guards Tank Army under Lieutenant General Pavel Rotmistrov as the only uncommitted armoured formation in the south, and it reached the Prokhorovka area on 11 July, its tanks having made a four-day dash from assembly areas almost 200 miles to the east. The army comprised the XVIII and XXIX Tank corps and the V Guards Mechanized Corps. Rotmistrov's 650 tanks were reinforced by the II Tank Corps and II Guards Tank Corps, increasing its strength to about 850 tanks, of which 500 were T-34s.

The massive clash of opposing armoured forces at Prokhorovka on 12 July marked the climax of Operation Citadel. On that day alone the Russians lost between 300 and 400 tanks and self-propelled guns destroyed or damaged; German losses were about eighty tanks and assault guns. The massive Soviet loss was due in part to Soviet tactics, which were often extraordinary, with battle groups of T-34s up to fifty strong charging headlong into the advancing Panzer formations, the Russians relying on their superior mobility to survive. As one account describes:

A Soviet attack by the 181st Tank Regiment was defeated by several SS Tigers, one of which, the 13th (Heavy) Company of the 1st SS Panzer Regiment, was commanded by Second Lieutenant Michael Wittmann, the most successful tank commander of the war. Wittmann's group was advancing in flank support of the German main attack when it was engaged by the Soviet tank regiment at long range. The Soviet charge, straight at the Tigers over open ground, was suicidal. The frontal armor of the Tiger was impervious to the 76mm guns of the T-34s at any great distance. The field was soon littered with burning T-34s ... None of the Tigers were lost, but the 181st Tank Regiment was annihilated.

Despite massive losses of Soviet armour, the German offensive slowed and finally halted. The SS Panzer divisions still had plenty of fight in them – in fact, on 14 July Panzer Division 'Das Reich' linked up with III Panzer Corps south of Prokhorovka and encircled several Soviet rifle divisions – but Hitler, having received news that the Allies had landed in Sicily, decided to cancel Citadel. Seizing their opportunity, the Russians quickly went over to the

Two German views of the battlefield at Kursk. These images give a good idea of the confusion that attended the fighting. (Bundesarchiv)

Kursk, July 1943. Soviet troops and T-34s advancing behind a creeping barrage. (Courtesy of Anthony Tucker-Jones)

A T-34 and infantry advancing under heavy shellfire at Kursk. (Novosti)

A T-34 Model 1943 advancing with infantry in support. (Courtesy of Anthony Tucker-Jones)

The Ilyushin Il-2 Sturmovik was the Soviet Air Force's principal ground-attack aircraft, and was used in huge numbers against German armour. (Robert Jackson archive)

A Henschel Hs 129B-3 anti-tank aircraft armed with a 75mm *Bordkanone*, the heaviest such weapon fitted to an aircraft. It was developed from the Pak 40 semi-automatic anti-tank gun. (Courtesy of Anthony Tucker-Jones)

Aleksandra Samusenko, who fought in the Battle of Kursk, was the only female tank commander in the First Guards Tank Army. She died of injuries sustained in an accident on 3 March 1945 and was buried at Lobez, Poland. (TASS)

offensive. Fresh reserves of armour brought the Soviet First Tank Army up to strength with 542 tanks and the Fifth Guards Tank Army to 503, but they continued to suffer fearsome losses. By the end of August the two Soviet tank armies had only 220 tanks between them, but Kharkov was recaptured on 22 August, and with that the German front gradually collapsed.

Throughout operations in the summer of 1943, battlefield air support played a key part. During the first three days of the fighting at Kursk, as the German Fourth Panzer Army drove a wedge twenty-five miles northward into the Kursk salient, its tanks and mechanized infantry came under continual air attack by Ilyushin IL-2 ground-attack aircraft, using PTAB hollow-charge anti-tank bombs, fragmentation and delayed-action bombs. These attacks slowed down the German thrust but failed to halt it, and when groups of T-34s attempted to attack the flanks of Fourth Panzer on 8 July they were subjected to assaults by Henschel Hs 129 ground-attack aircraft armed with 30mm cannon, firing at the tanks' vulnerable rear areas. Many tanks were knocked out and the remainder withdrew in confusion, their accompanying infantry being harassed by Focke-Wulf Fw 190 fighter-bombers dropping fragmentation bombs.

The Henschel Hs 129 was only one tool in the Luftwaffe's arsenal of anti-tank aircraft. Almost as soon as Operation Barbarossa was launched in 1941, and the Wehrmacht came up against the first T-34s, it had become clear that a dedicated low-level attack aircraft was needed to support the ground forces. It was hoped that the Junkers Ju 87D would meet the requirement, armed with free-fall armour-piercing ammunition, but this was soon replaced by the concept of a fast, heavily armoured aircraft fitted with heavy cannon. As the harsh winter conditions on the Eastern Front often prevented anti-tank guns from being brought up in time to repulse Soviet armoured attacks, and because of the sheer scale of operations, mobile tank reserves could not be redeployed in time to oppose enemy armour.

Early in 1943, a variant of the Junkers Ju 87 Stuka, the Ju 87G, appeared on the Russian front to undertake operational trials with a special unit, Panzerjagdkommando Weiss, commanded by Oberstleutnant Otto Weiss, which formed at Bryansk. Fitted with extra armour, it was armed with two large 37mm Flak 18 anti-tank cannon. Each 37mm gun had a magazine holding twelve tungsten-cored armour-piercing shells, capable of penetrating 58mm (2.3in) of armour at a 60° angle of impact from a range of 100m (328ft).

The Ju 87G, based on the Ju 87D-3, was developed at Rechlin, the Luftwaffe's experimental establishment in northern Germany, much of the trial work being carried out by the famous Stuka ace Oberleutnant Hans-Ulrich Rudel. The first converted aircraft were used against Soviet landing craft in the Black Sea, and with great success. In the space of three weeks, Rudel himself destroyed seventy such boats, and in March 1943 he destroyed a T-34 with the new aircraft. By the end of the war, Rudel had amassed a total of 402 Soviet tanks destroyed, the majority while flying the cannon-armed Stuka.

Although the main threat to the T-34 continued to be artillery and air attack, in the second half of 1943 the Russians began to encounter increasing numbers of hand-held infantry anti-tank weapons. One was the Panzerschreck (Tank Terror), a copy of the American bazooka; another the Faustpatrone (Fist Cartridge), which was developed into the Panzerfaust (Tank Fist), a weapon much more effective against the T-34's sloped armour. A cheap, single-shot recoilless weapon handled by a single soldier,

Panzerfaust consisted of a small disposable pre-loaded launch tube firing a high-explosive shaped charge anti-tank warhead. As its effective range was only about 200 feet (60m) its use required considerable courage on the part of its operator. Some six million were produced by the end of the war, and the later versions were capable of penetrating 200mm of armour.

After the battle of Kursk, the Germans were never again in a position to launch a strategic offensive. By mid-September 1943 the Soviet Southern and Southwestern fronts had driven the enemy from the Donets basin, and on the 22nd of that month the Dnieper was reached by the Third Guards Tank Army. On 6 November the Russians recaptured Kiev after bitter fighting, and Soviet forces crossed the Dnieper at a number of other points. Further north, the Central Front under General Konstantin Rokossovsky breached the river and reached the Pripet marshes, while the Western Front recaptured Smolensk and drove on towards Vitebsk.

Top: The Junkers Ju 87G Stuka, armed with two 37mm high-velocity cannon, was the Luftwaffe's main tank-killer on the Eastern Front. Its chief exponent was Hans-Ulrich Rudel, who destroyed over 400 Russian tanks. (Robert Jackson archive)

Centre: The 50mm Pak 38 was one of the very few early anti-tank guns capable of penetrating the T-34's armour.

Above: A T-34/76 Model 1943. The tank now features a commander's cupola. (Bundesarchiv)

Top: A T-34/85 preserved at the Museé des Blindés, Saumur.

Above: Soviet troops riding T-34/85s into battle. (Courtesy of Anthony Tucker-Jones)

mounting a much more powerful gun. This was the long 85mm ZIS C-53 which, like the German 88mm, was adapted from an anti-aircraft gun and used the same ammunition. Its performance was roughly similar to that of the 88mm Tiger I; the 85mm fired a 21.5lb shot at a muzzle velocity of 3,600ft/sec, compared with the 88mm gun's 22.25lb shot at 2,657ft/sec. The 85mm gun had a maximum elevation of plus 25° and its normal range was 5,200 yards.

Production of the modified T-34 began in February 1944, and by May the production level had reached 1,200 tanks per month.

As soon as the new variant was identified by the Germans, they applied the designation T-34/85 to it, the earlier models being collectively known as the T-34/76. These designations were never used by the Russians, although they subsequently passed into common usage.

As usual with modified designs, there was a penalty to pay. The T-34/85's heavier gun, coupled with in increased armour, added up to a heavier tank, which meant a certain loss of operational flexibility. Its overall weight rose from 27 to 32 tons, and its effective range dropped from 280 miles to about 190. Nevertheless, when it entered production in the winter of 1943–44, the T-34/85 was the most formidable tank in the world. It was the tank that would lead the Red Army to the gates of Berlin.

Statistics:	T-34/85
Armament:	85mm (3.35in) ZiS-S-53 gun, two 7.62mm (0.3in) DT MGs
Armour:	90mm (3.54in)
Crew:	5
Dimensions:	Length 8.15m (26ft 7in); Width 2.99m (9ft 7in); Height 2.74m (9ft)
Weight:	32,000kg (31.5 tons)
Powerplant:	V-2-34 12-cylinder diesel, 373kW (500bhp) at 1,800rpm
Speed:	55kph (34mph)
Range:	300km (190 miles)

During 1943 the Soviet armoured forces were joined by Czech and Polish tank brigades, armed with the T-34 Model 1943 and a variety of lighter tanks. The Czech brigade first went into action during the Battle of Kiev in November and captured the city centre.

The stage was now set for a succession of massive Russian offensives that would be launched in 1944, and the T-34 would again be at the forefront – although now it was a T-34 of a different kind, far more effective than the models that had confronted the Germans in the previous year.

Enter the T-34/85

It was in October 1942 that Russian forces on the Leningrad Front had first come face to face with the formidable Tiger I, whose 100mm frontal armour was proof against the Russians' 76.2mm anti-tank guns and whose 80mm side armour could only be penetrated only from the closest range. Fortunately for the Russians, the massive new 56-ton Panzers were few in number, production only having started in August, and the Tiger Mk I was plagued by technical problems. Nevertheless, the appearance of the Tiger precipitated a race that would see huge advances in armour and gunnery during 1943.

The Soviet response was to upgrade the T-34, making far-reaching changes to the existing design to produce a more effective fighting vehicle. The existing T-34 chassis was adapted to take a cast, three-man turret

In April and May 1944 the Russians liberated the Crimea. It was the last major operation before the main Soviet offensive of 1944, the object of which was the destruction of German Army Group Centre. Centred on Minsk, this army group, which was under the command of Field Marshal Model, comprised the Second, Fourth and Ninth armies and the Third Panzer Army – a total of fifty divisions, with 1,000 tanks and 1.2 million men. For air support, the Luftwaffe had managed to scrape together about 1,400 combat aircraft.

The destruction of Army Group Centre would not only result in the expulsion of German forces from the Soviet Union: the army group was defending what amounted to a broad highway that led into the heart of central Europe, and if Model's forces were smashed that highway would be left wide open. In readiness for the offensive, the Russians assembled over 2.5 million men on four fronts, stretching in a huge arc from north to south.

Early in June, a matter of days after the Allied landings in Normandy, the Russians struck their first blow, in effect a preliminary to the main offensive. The attack was launched against the Soviet Union's old adversary, Finland, now an ally of Germany. On 4 September 1944 the Finns were forced into an armistice with the Russians for the second time in five years, and under the terms of this armistice they turned their weapons on their former allies, who were now withdrawing into Norway and the Baltic states. During this brief conflict the Finnish Army made use of a small number of T-34s, the first of which had been captured during the early fighting in 1941.

The main Soviet offensive in Byelorussia, codenamed Operation Bagration after Prince Pyotr Ivanovich Bagration, an Imperial Russian general mortally wounded at Borodino in 1812, began at dawn on 22 June 1944, three years to the day, and almost to the minute, since the launch of Operation Barbarossa. The first attacks were directed against three key German strongpoints at Vitebsk, Mogilev and Bobruisk. After an intense air and artillery bombardment, two Soviet armies succeeded in linking up west of Vitebsk on 25 June, and the fortress itself fell two days later. The following day Mogilev was also captured, but at such appalling cost to the Russians that the Second Byelorussian Front was unable to continue the offensive until strong reinforcements arrived. The greatest initial success came on the First Byelorussian Front, where – under the brilliant leadership of General Rokossovsky – the Russians isolated part of the German Ninth Army around Bobruisk. The trapped German forces surrendered on 29 June.

By 13 July, the Soviet high command had achieved its primary aim: the German Army Group Centre had virtually ceased to exist. The German retreat continued throughout August, by which time the Russians had forced their way to the borders of East Prussia. The First and Second Byelorussian fronts had already reached the river Bug in July and captured Lublin, subsequently launching a new thrust towards the Vistula and Warsaw.

Meanwhile, the German Army Group North found itself in grave danger. Following the success of Operation Bagration, the Russians launched a massive assault which effectively isolated the army group in a pocket in Coerland (Latvia) and almost succeeded in breaking through to the Gulf of Riga. To counter the threat, Panzerverband von Strachwitz was hastily reformed from elements of the 101st Panzer

Brigade (Colonel Meinrad von Lauchert) and the newly formed SS Panzer Brigade Gross (SS Sturmbannführer Gross). Inside the pocket, the remaining tanks and self-propelled guns of the Hermann von Salza and the last of Jähde's Tigers were formed into another battle group.

On 19 August, 1944, both armoured formations launched a simultaneous assault from inside and outside the pocket, and succeeded in restoring contact between Strachwitz and the remnants of the Nordland Division. This operation was effectively supported by the heavy cruiser *Prinz Eugen*, now with the Baltic Fleet Training Squadron, whose eight-inch shells destroyed forty-eight T-34s assembling in the town square at Tukkum on the Gulf of Riga. It was an extremely effective demonstration of what artillery fire – or in this case naval gunfire – could achieve against a mass of enemy armour.

In September 1944 the Russians occupied Romania and Bulgaria. In the following month they captured Belgrade and moved northwestward into Hungary to begin a winter offensive aginst the German and Hungarian armies which were still fighting hard. By mid-December, 180,000 German and Hungarian troops were besieged in Budapest. At the turn of the year, the front ran from Yugoslavia to the Baltic, cutting across Poland and Czechoslovakia and running along the border of East Prussia. For the final thrust that would take them into the heart of Germany, the Russians had assembled nearly five million men

Top: Soviet troops debarking from a T-34 with the tank still in motion (via Tom Cooper)

Above: T-34/76 Model 1943 of the Polish Armoured Brigade, preserved as a museum piece in Poznan. Note the hexagonal turret. (Radomil, public domain)

T-34/85 of the 36th Guards Tank Brigade in Yugoslavia, October 1944. (TASS)

T-34s and support troops of the 3rd Polish Tank Brigade. (Sovfoto)

Journey's end: a T-34 in Berlin, May 1945, with the Brandenburg Gate in the background. (Novosti, via Tom Cooper)

divided among forty-five field armies, eleven Guards armies, five shock armies and six tank armies, all covered by a vast air umbrella of 17,000 combat aircraft of thirteen air armies.

While Zhukov and Koniev were preparing for the thrust to Berlin, the Soviet forces in East Prussia were engaged in bitter fighting as they systematically destroyed each centre of German resistance. In March, the exceptionally strong German defensive position at Heilsberg was eliminated and the Russians now turned their attention to Königsberg, where 130,000 Germans were holding one of the mightiest fortresses in Europe. For two weeks, 2,000 Soviet bombers hammered the bastion from end to end, and early in April four Soviet divisions launched their attack, suffering staggering casualties before the garrison was overwhelmed.

During the last week of March 1945 the Soviet forces in the south broke through to the Austrian border, and on 7 April they were fighting for Vienna. Soon afterwards they joined up with the Americans at Linz, completing the Allied ring around southern Germany. The focus now shifted to the so-called Oder-Neisse line, where Zhukov

and Koniev had completed their defences. Along the two rivers, a massive force of 1,600,000 men, 41,000 guns and 630 tanks stood ready for the assault.

At dawn on 8 April the Russians launched a massive air onslaught on the German defences west of the Oder and Neisse rivers. Then, in the wake of one of the biggest artillery barrages in history, masses of Soviet shock troops stormed the first line of enemy defences on the Seelow Heights. The Germans fought back fanatically, and it took the Russians two days to advance over the five miles to the second line of defences. German resistance was less fierce both here and at the third line of defence, and within a week Zhukov's forces had broken through and smashed the German Ninth Army.

For the Russians, though, it had been a costly undertaking. On the first day of the assault on the Seelow Heights they lost seventy-five tanks, mostly T-34s, with 2,250 men killed and 3,400 wounded, and on the second day the first wave of fifty T-34s was utterly destroyed by artillery, air attack and Panzerfausts. The second assault wave fared no better, with thirty-four T-34s knocked out. On average, the Russians lost ninety-two tanks per day before the Seelow Heights were secured on 11 April. Again, the majority were T-34s.

On 21 April came the news that the elite Eighth Guards Army under General Chuikov was fighting in the suburbs of Berlin. It was a fitting triumph for the old campaigner who had withstood the German onslaught on Stalingrad more than two years earlier.

In August 1945, three months after Germany's surrender, it was the T-34 that spearheaded the Soviet assault on Japanese-occupied Manchuria. That swift campaign brought the Second World War to a close, but five years later the T-34 would again see combat in the Far East.

The T-34 in action after the Second World War

The T-34 medium tank remained in production throughout the Second World War. By the end of 1945 over 57,300 T-34s had been built, of which 34,780 were the T-34/76 version and 22,559 the T-34/85. A further 2,701 T-34s were built in the Soviet Union after the war, and the tank was built under licence in Poland and Czechoslovakia, these countries producing 1,380 and 3,185 examples respectively. The T-34 chassis also served as the basis for 13,170 self-propelled guns. The biggest T-34 producer was Factory No. 183 (the Ural Tank Factory), which built 28,952 T-34s of both types from 1941 to 1945; the second was the Krasnoye Sormovo Factory No. 112 in Gorky, which produced 12,604. By the war's end, the T-34 accounted for some 55 per cent of Soviet tank production.

Outside the USSR, Czechoslovakia was the main post-war manufacturer of the T-34. Following the country's subordination to the Soviet Union, the later supplied some T-34 components in 1951, and after these were assembled and the complete tanks tested, licence production started in February 1952 and continued until the end of 1956, by which time 2,736 T-34/85s had been manufactured. About half the Czech-built T-34s were destined for export.

In all, the T-34 served with the armoured forces of forty nations. In addition to the Soviet Union's Warsaw Pact allies, the tank was supplied to many of the USSR's client states. Among the foremost was North Korea, which deployed a brigade of about 120 T-34s to spearhead its invasion of South Korea in June 1950. The T-34s enjoyed early successes against American M24 Chaffee light tanks, and the 2.36-inch bazooka was useless against their armour, but by the end of August 1950 a combination of recently arrived M26 Pershing tanks and overwhelming air superiority gave the United Nations forces the advantage, and when the UN landing at Inchon in September forced the North Koreans to retreat many T-34s had to be abandoned for lack of fuel. A post-war assessment revealed that the North Koreans lost 239 T-34s and seventy-four Su-76 SP guns as their forces were cleared from South Korea, ninety-seven of them in tank-v-tank engagements.

The People's Republic of China (PRC) deployed four regiments of tanks, mostly T-34/85s, to Korea when it entered the conflict in February 1951, but combats between these and UN tanks were few. The People's Liberation Army (PLA) had begun to received T-34s from the Soviet Union in 1949; the number delivered eventually totalled 1,837 of both variants, and the

A North Korean T-34 knocked out by US forces, September 1950. (Courtesy of Anthony Tucker-Jones)

The M26 Pershing was hurriedly shipped to Korea to counter the T-34, and soon proved more than a match for it. (Courtesy of Anthony Tucker-Jones)

The T-34/85 manufactured in the Chinese People's Republic was known as the Type 58. This example came to grief in Korea (Source unknown)

A Bosnian Serb T-34/85 abandoned during the 1990s conflict in the Balkans. The rubber matting was intended to hide its thermal signature. (Paalso, public domain)

Cuban T-34/84, fitted with a mine plough, abandoned in Angola.

This T-100 tank destroyer variant, based on the T-34 chassis, was armed with a 100mm D10-S gun. This captured example is seen in Yad la-Shiryon Museum, Israel. The vehicle next to it is an IS-3 heavy tank.

A Syrian T-34/85 on the Golan Heights, 1967. (Tom Cooper)

Even today, T-34s continue to emerge from bogs and swamps in eastern and northern Europe. This example, a captured T-34/76 with German markings, was pulled from a lake in Estonia. (Rense.com News Service)

Chinese soon developed their own copy of the T-34/85 under the designation Type 58, which was replaced by the Type 59, a Chinese version of the Soviet T-54A main battle tank (MBT).

Egypt was a major user of the T-34, receiving the first of 820 Czech-built T-34/85s in 1953. The Egyptian T-34s saw action during the Six-Day War of 1956, operating in support of the Egyptian Army's infantry divisions. One of the main actions was fought at Abu Ageila, when sixty-six T-34s engaged Israeli armoured forces pushing into central Sinai. The T-34s proved no match for the Israelis' modern AMX-13, Centurion and Super Sherman tanks and forty were destroyed. The Israeli loss was nineteen tanks, mostly knocked out by Egyptian SU-100 tank destroyers, twenty-two of which were used in the battle. Syria also received 120 T-34/85s, which were annihilated in fighting around the Golan Heights.

Cuba, where a communist regime was established after 1959, received many T-34 tanks as part of an arms supply deal with the Soviet Union, and the then Cuban dictator Fidel Castro famously entered Havana riding one following the Bay of Pigs invasion by Cuban exiles in 1961, when counter-revolutionary forces were defeated. Many Cuban T-34s found their way to Angola and were used in the series of bitter civil wars that raged there for twenty-seven years following the end of Portuguese colonial rule in 1974. Other T-34s came directly from the Soviet Union, raising the total deployed to around 120. Some were destroyed by South African Air Force Buccaneer strike aircraft, armed with 68mm SNEB rockets, and Mirage IIICZs attacking the tanks' vulnerable areas with 30mm cannon fire.

In more recent times, small numbers of T-34/85s have been used in limited conflicts, including Bosnia in the 1990s and the Yemen in 2015. Like an old soldier, it seems that the T-34 refuses to die, but rather fades away.